INTERNATIONAL DEVELOPMENT IN FOCUS

Essays on Equity, Health, and Education in Sierra Leone

Selected Challenges and Benefits

ALEJANDRO DE LA FUENTE, ELIZABETH M. FOSTER, AND
QUENTIN WODON, EDITORS

Contents

Boxes

Figures

Tables

Acknowledgments

The team gratefully acknowledges Andrew Dabalen, Henry Kerali, Gayle Martin, Meskerem Mulatu, and Pierella Paci for their overall guidance and support in the preparation of the notes that comprise this volume.

We also thank the following colleagues for their support in publishing this volume: Abdu Muwonge, Johan A. Mistiaen, Scherezad Joya Monami Latif, Patrick M. Mullen, Mari Shojo, Namrata Raman Tognatta, Rose Mungai, Paul Corral, Dena Ringold, Pierre Laporte, Elena Glinskaya, Magnus Lindelow, Lydia Mesfin Asseres, Agata Pawlowska, Nicolas Rosemberg, and Anne Tully.

We especially thank the following coauthors who contributed to different pieces contained in the volume: Antonio Giuffrida, Hanan Jacoby, Chata Male, Adenike Onagoruwa, and Mari Shojo. We are also thankful to the following peer reviewers for their comments and feedback: Tom Bundervoet, Minh Cong Nguyen, David Evans, Deon Filmer, Antonio Giuffrida, Junko Onishi, Carlos Rodriguez Castelan, and Emmanuel Skoufias.

The team greatly benefited from conversations with and comments from Kathleen Beegle, Parminder Brar, Errol Graham, Kristen Himelein, Kazumi Inden, and Kemoh Mansaray.

We are grateful to Prof. Osman Sankoh for granting the team access to the 2018 Sierra Leone Integrated Household Survey and the 2019 Free Quality Education Mobile Phone Survey, both conducted by Statistics Sierra Leone with support from the World Bank. We also thank the Ministry of Basic and Senior Secondary Education for granting us access to the 2018 Annual School Census, which was conducted in conjunction with Statistics Sierra Leone.

Our special appreciation goes to our colleagues Thanh Thi Mai, Polycarp Otieno, and Mari Shojo, who provided the school census data and invaluable conversations enabling us to understand the Free Quality School Education Program. We are also grateful to Siobhan Murray, Arthur Shaw, and Abubakarr Turay for their assistance at different stages during the design and implementation of the Free Quality Education Mobile Phone Survey.

About the Editors

Alejandro de la Fuente is a senior economist in the World Bank's Poverty and Equity Global Practice. His work has focused on low- and middle-income countries, including in fragile settings in West and Southern Africa, East and South Asia, and Latin America. His current work involves providing high-quality analytics on poverty, program evaluation, and risk and vulnerability, as well as policy guidance and hands-on support to World Bank operations on social protection. Previous experience includes working for other multilateral organizations (the United Nations Development Programme, the United Nations Office for Disaster Risk Reduction, and the Inter-American Development Bank) and as a public servant at the Ministry of Social Development and the Office of the President in Mexico. He has published several articles in peer-reviewed journals and has coauthored or coedited five books. He holds a DPhil degree in development studies and development economics from Oxford University.

Elizabeth M. Foster is an economist in the World Bank's Poverty and Equity Global Practice in West and Central Africa. She lived in Sierra Leone for over 15 years while working for the World Bank and various nongovernmental organizations and research organizations. Her work focuses on the welfare dynamics of households in the Sahel region and the best practice for measurement of poverty using both international and national measures. She holds a BA degree in mathematics from Harvard University and a master's degree in public affairs from Princeton University.

Quentin Wodon is the director of the United Nations Educational, Scientific and Cultural Organization's International Institute for Capacity Building in Africa. Previously, he worked for 24 years at the World Bank, including as lead economist, lead poverty specialist, and manager of the unit on values and development. Before that, he taught with tenure at the University of Namur. He has also taught at Addis Ababa University, American University, and Georgetown University. A business engineering graduate, after an assignment in Asia as laureate of a prize, he worked in brand management for Procter & Gamble. He then shifted careers to join a nonprofit organization working with the extreme poor population, which led him to pursue a career in international development. He has over 700 publications and has worked on policy issues across sectors in more than 60 countries. He holds PhD degrees in economics, environmental science, health sciences, and theology.

Abbreviations

ASC	Annual School Census
DHS	Demographic and Health Survey
EA	enumeration area
FQEMPS	Free Quality Education Mobile Phone Survey
FQSE	Free Quality School Education Program
GDP	gross domestic product
HCI	Human Capital Index
JSS	junior secondary school
MICS	Multi-Indicator Cluster Survey
ODA	official development assistance
PPP	purchasing power parity
SLIHS	Sierra Leone Integrated Household Survey
SRH	sexual and reproductive health
SSS	senior secondary school

1 Introduction

ALEJANDRO DE LA FUENTE, ELIZABETH M. FOSTER, AND QUENTIN WODON

OVERVIEW

Human capital is essential for growth and poverty reduction. It also accounts for two-thirds of the changing wealth of nations. Life-cycle approaches to human development emphasize the importance of investing along the life cycle. Early childhood development, especially during the first 1,000 days of a child's life, fundamentally affects individuals' future development and productivity. Thereafter, schooling and, even more important, learning affect the ability of individuals to find decent work. The returns on schooling are high, especially at the postprimary level. Education also has major impacts on a wide range of outcomes, especially for girls; these impacts range from fertility to decision-making ability in the household, as well as the risk of intimate partner violence. Being educated is also valuable in itself, because it can improve the quality of people's lives in ways beyond income-enhancing productivity.

Over the past few years, teams at the World Bank explored various aspects of human capital in Sierra Leone using a range of data sources. This edited volume puts together a number of contributions to make them more widely available and provide access to some of the background work that informed World Bank reports, including a recent Economic Update with a focus on educating girls and ending child marriage. This introduction briefly summarizes some of the key findings from the analyses.

Sierra Leone, like other countries in West Africa, is still facing a difficult post-COVID-19 pandemic recovery due to concurrent domestic and external shocks. Estimated gross domestic product growth for 2022 was nearly 3 percent, marking a reversal of the encouraging rebound observed in 2021, when gross domestic product grew by 4.1 percent following a 2 percent contraction in 2020. Headline inflation averaged 27 percent in 2022, compared to 12 percent the previous year. Despite a decrease in global food and fuel prices, inflation worsened owing to the depreciation of the leone (60 percent during 2022) and loose fiscal policies.[1] Even before the pandemic, Sierra Leone was one of the poorest countries within Sub-Saharan Africa, with a gross national income per capita of US$500 in 2018. The country ranked near the bottom of all countries in the Human Development Index and also performed poorly in the World Bank's Human Capital Index. The latter index is based on five indicators: probability of survival to age five,

TABLE 1.1 **Human Capital Index, Sierra Leone and Sub-Saharan Africa, 2020**

INDICATOR	SIERRA LEONE	SUB-SAHARAN AFRICA
Probability of survival to age 5	0.89	0.93
Expected years of school	9.6	8.3
Harmonized test scores	316	374
Children under 5 not stunted (%)	0.71	0.69
Survival rate from ages 15 to 60	0.63	0.74
Human Capital Index	**0.36**	**0.40**

Source: World Bank Human Capital Index.

expected years of schooling, harmonized test scores, children under five not stunted, and adult survival. The values of those indicators are provided in table 1.1 for Sierra Leone and for Sub-Saharan Africa as a whole.

Despite these low rankings, in the years since the end of the civil war in 2002, there has been notable progress. The return to peace and stability and the ample availability of fertile land facilitated recovery and growth in agriculture. Urban areas have become local trading and commercial centers, and the capital Freetown has seen many sources of new wealth and development (World Bank Group 2018). Poverty significantly declined from 2003 to 2011. Progress continued, although less emphatically, until 2018, and access to basic services improved, particularly in education and health.

Sierra Leone has made strides in key indicators on education and health. Although 2018 was the first year the Human Capital Index was formally calculated, data on education indicators have been collected for a number of years on household surveys such as the Multi-Indicator Cluster Survey and the Sierra Leone Integrated Household Survey. For instance, the expected years of schooling increased from 8.5 years in 2003 to 9.7 in 2018. The primary completion rate almost doubled from 34 percent in 2003 to 66 percent in 2018. However, improvements in some of these dimensions should not distract policy makers from the challenges posed by the relative lack of progress in others. Moreover, improvements have not always permeated the entire population. The rural poor, in particular, have faced relative lack of progress in some of those same services, such as access to secondary education.

THE ORGANIZATION OF THIS BOOK

Chapter 2 of this book explores the evolution of poverty and inequality between 2011 and 2018, a very turbulent period in the country's history owing to the Ebola outbreak and the collapse in iron ore prices. It finds that Sierra Leone managed a modest reduction in monetary poverty, with urban areas driving the reduction. The analysis in the chapter also reveals a number of troubling factors as the country seeks to eliminate extreme poverty and achieve middle-income status. The two most important are an increase in inequality and the failure to reduce extreme poverty. The country's monetary poverty remains high and did not lessen in rural areas between 2011 and 2018. Furthermore, extreme poverty increased significantly in small towns and rural areas and the eastern provinces. If the current pattern of growth is continued, extreme poverty will not be eliminated by 2039 and may, in fact, increase. The country would also become increasingly divided between a prospering urban population and an increasingly deprived rural population.

Chapters 3 and 4 set out to explore and understand whether progress happened on nonmonetary dimensions of poverty, particularly on proper health and education, which are central to long-term poverty reduction in Sierra Leone. Good health and educational attainment among children are some of the main factors that may remove poverty over a child's life and across generations.

Strong gains in under-five and maternal mortality, as well as stunting in children since the end of the war, have tended to be pro-poor. A strong convergence is seen in under-five and infant mortality rates over time, with disadvantaged groups seeing the most progress and closing the gap. The results for stunting are less dramatic, but households in the middle of the wealth distribution have been catching up with the top, and the gap between children of mothers with different education levels has been closing. These gains in health outcomes for the most disadvantaged children can be explained at least in part by strong improvements in the use of antenatal care and assisted delivery for the most disadvantaged women. Less improvement, either overall or in terms of closing the gap between different groups of households, is seen for early childbearing, contraceptive use, childhood vaccinations, and physical access to clinics (use of these services will reduce maternal mortality as well as child mortality). Most households report paying something for antenatal care and treatment of sick children, even at government health facilities, despite these services being officially free under the Free Health Care Initiative.

As discussed earlier, despite strong progress in education outcomes since the end of the war in 2001, Sierra Leone ranks near the bottom of the World Bank's Human Capital Index. Understanding whether this progress has been shared across all kinds of households or whether certain groups have been left behind will be crucial in supporting further progress in human capital development. Gains in education indicators (expected years of schooling and primary school completion) during the past couple of decades are observed among households concentrated in the middle of the income distribution that catch up with households located at the top of the distribution. In fact, the biggest gains for households occur in the middle of the income distribution and in urban areas outside the capital city. A small difference between girls and boys in expected years of schooling has closed. Access to schools and school expenses remain important barriers to education. Up until 2018, there had been no improvement in access to primary schools for poor and rural households, and a wide gap remains in access to secondary schools. Lack of perceived usefulness is also an important barrier, cited frequently by households as the main reason children fail to start school or drop out.

Chapter 5 examines the immediate effects of the flagship program of the current government—the Free Quality School Education Program (FQSE)—on enrollment and out-of-pocket expenditures of households, using data collected just after the first term of the program, covering the education of children in the household for the first terms of 2017–18 and 2018–19. For most children, the school attended both years can be linked to the annual school census to determine their eligibility to receive fee subsidy grants for the first term. The authors find a very small effect of FQSE on enrollment, mostly from a modest increase in the number of five-to-seven-year-olds starting school concentrated among the poorer households. By contrast, the impact on school fee expenditures is large, with 90 percent of beneficiary schools and a large number of nonbeneficiary public schools eliminating school fees. Benefits from FQSE are lowest for the poorest (quintile of) households, largely because of their lower enrollment rates, especially in secondary school, as well as their lower access to beneficiary schools. However, as a percentage of income, FQSE benefits are highest for the poorest households.

Chapter 6 discusses the need to invest in adolescent girls by educating girls and ending child marriage. As elsewhere in West Africa, adolescent girls in Sierra Leone continue to have relatively high rates of child marriage and early childbearing and low educational attainment. Based on data from the 2019 Demographic and Health Survey, 27.1 percent of girls ages 18–22 married as children and 27.3 percent had their first child before they were 18. In part, as a result, less than half of girls complete lower-secondary education. For upper-secondary education, the completion rate is about one-fifth. These risks tend to be magnified in times of crisis, including in the context of the recent COVID-19 pandemic. Although gains have been made in recent decades, the rate of progress is much too slow for Sierra Leone to achieve the targets adopted under the Sustainable Development Goals.

To conclude, beyond its natural resources, Sierra Leone's most substantial asset is its young and dynamic population. The 2015 Population and Housing Census found that Sierra Leone had an average population growth rate of 3.2 percent between 2004 and 2015. Forty-one percent of the population is under 15. Human capital is truly a key resource for the country. It must be nurtured for the wide range of benefits that it generates and for Sierra Leone to achieve its full potential. It is hoped that the analyses provided in this volume will be useful to policy makers and practitioners, as well as other researchers, in thinking about ways to reduce poverty and improve human capital and development outcomes in Sierra Leone.

NOTE

1. Refer to "The World Bank in Sierra Leone," https://www.worldbank.org/en/country/sierraleone/overview.

REFERENCE

World Bank Group. 2018. "Republic of Sierra Leone: Priorities for Sustainable Growth and Poverty Reduction—Systematic Country Diagnostic." World Bank Group, Washington, DC. http://documents.worldbank.org/curated/en/152711522893772195/Sierra-Leone-Systematic-Country-Diagnostic-Priorities-for-Sustainable-Growth-and-Poverty-Reduction.

2 Poverty and Shared Prosperity in Sierra Leone, 2011–18

ALEJANDRO DE LA FUENTE AND ELIZABETH M. FOSTER

INTRODUCTION

Sierra Leone is a country in Western Africa with a highly advantageous geography and abundant renewable and nonrenewable natural resources. The country possesses significant renewable natural resource endowments in land, forests, and fisheries. Almost 75 percent of the total land area is arable, and rainfall and sunlight are abundant. The country's rainfall, soil, sunlight, and river basins endow the country with highly naturally fertile land that is considered suitable for a wide variety of food and cash crops with potentially high crop yields. With more than 400 kilometers of coastline, Sierra Leone has abundant and varied fish resources. The country is also well endowed with mineral resources—extensive alluvial and kimberlitic diamonds, bauxite, rutile, and gold deposits, as well as large quantities of iron ore.

The country's population is young, diverse, urbanizing, and rapidly growing. According to the 2015 Population and Housing Census, the population of Sierra Leone is approximately 7.1 million, with 41 percent of the population under the age of 15 and 75 percent below the age of 35; and the total fertility rate is 5.2 children per woman. The 2015 census also found that Sierra Leone had an average population growth rate of 3.2 percent between 2004 and 2015. The share of the population living in urban areas nearly doubled, from 21 percent in 1967 to almost 40 percent in 2015, with a high concentration in the capital, Freetown, which has grown to a population of more than 1 million. Almost 60 percent of the working-age population is self-employed in agriculture, and another 28.6 percent is self-employed in other sectors.

Sierra Leone capitalized on these factors to experience a steady increase in per capita income from 2001 to 2014, its longest period since obtaining independence in 1961. Per capita gross domestic product (GDP) went from stagnating in the period from independence to the civil war to contracting an average of 3.4 percent per year between 1991 and 2001 (civil war) to increasing an average of 5.9 percent per year from 2002 to 2014 (post–civil war period). Economic growth was driven mainly by agriculture. Between 2001 and 2014, agriculture (including livestock, forestry, and fisheries) grew by an average of 8 percent per year, contributing almost 50 percent to the total increase in real GDP over this period. According to data from the Food and Agriculture Organization of the United Nations, crop production increased by an average of 12.5 percent per year during the period, driven mainly by an increase in land use and, to a lesser extent, improvement in yield per hectare. Industry was the second-largest contributor to growth, driven mainly by two large-scale iron ore mining projects that began production in 2011. Services increased by 5.8 percent per year during this period.

Sierra Leone's period of steady growth ended in 2015, as the country was severely affected by the twin shocks of the Ebola outbreak in 2014 and the downturn in international iron ore prices. The economy contracted by more than 20 percent owing to the spread of the Ebola epidemic and to both iron ore mining operations ceasing production because of low international prices. Iron production declined by 84 percent in 2014, and growth in the rest of the economy slowed to near zero, with the services sector being particularly hard-hit. Growth resumed in 2016, following the end of the Ebola outbreak and the return to operation of the largest iron ore mine.

This chapter seeks to understand whether the growth episodes of the country and its history of recurrent shocks since the turn of the century have affected development outcomes over the years, particularly poverty and inequality. After a discussion of the data and methodology used, the subsequent section on results first provides a profile of monetary poverty (both absolute and extreme) and inequality in Sierra Leone as of 2018. The spatial distribution of poverty (both by district and by rural versus urban areas) is presented, as is the correlation between poverty and various household characteristics. Sierra Leone is also compared to Sub-Saharan African countries using the international poverty line.

The results section then describes how poverty and inequality changed between 2011 and 2018 (poverty trends are in fact traced back to 2003). Changes in poverty are presented for absolute poverty and extreme poverty, poverty rates, and total number of poor, nationally and for urban versus rural areas. Growth incidence curves are constructed with the growth rate for various segments of the population, including for the bottom 40 percent (to proxy the shared prosperity indicator). Changes in poverty are decomposed in two ways: (1) into contributions from changing household characteristics (urban versus rural, education level) and changing poverty rates for different types of households, and (2) into contributions from growth and changing inequality. Overall changes in inequality between 2011 and 2018 are also presented. The final section presents conclusions.

DATA AND METHODOLOGY

Statistics Sierra Leone and its partners have been collecting nationally representative household survey data since 2003 through the Sierra Leone Integrated Household Survey (SLIHS).[1] This survey covers a wide range of social and economic topics and is the primary source for estimations of poverty within the country; it provides information on other indicators for the National Development Plan.

Statistics Sierra Leone has conducted three rounds of the SLIHS, in 2003–04, 2011, and 2018, which are the primary data sets used for this chapter. In each case, data collection took place over a 12-month period. The SLIHS 2018 was conducted from January to December 2018 and covered 6,840 households.

It used the 2015 Population and Housing Census as the sampling frame. The households were clustered at the level of census enumeration area (EA), with 684 EAs selected and 10 households per EA surveyed. The sample was stratified by district (using the 14 districts defined as of the 2015 census) and urban/rural areas. The SLIHS 2011 was conducted from January to December 2011 and covered 6,727 households. It used the 2004 Population and Housing Census as the sampling frame. The households were clustered at the level of census EA, with 684 EAs selected and 10 households per EA targeted (final total sample size: 6,727 households). The sample was stratified by local council (14 district councils and 5 city councils) and urban/rural areas within district councils. The SLIHS 2003–04 was conducted between April 2003 and March 2004. It used the 1985 census as the sampling frame. The households were clustered at the level of census EA, with 160 rural EAs and 132 urban EAs selected and 10 households per rural EA and 15 households per urban EA targeted (final sample size: 3,714 households). The sample was stratified by province (using the four provinces before 2017) and by urban versus rural

Poverty analysis requires three main elements. The first is a welfare indicator (consumption in the analysis presented in this chapter) that can be used to compare the well-being of individuals or households. The second is a poverty line that can be compared against the welfare indicator to ascertain the poverty status of households and individuals. Last, a way (or ways) to aggregate these comparisons to produce overall measures of poverty (such as the national poverty rate) is needed.

Two poverty lines are defined: The *food poverty line* is the amount needed (per adult equivalent) to purchase food following local diet patterns that provides sufficient calories (defined as 2,700 for Sierra Leone). The *total poverty line* is the food poverty line plus a nonfood allowance that considers the basic nonfood needs of the population. Based on these lines, and the level of consumption, three definitions of being poor are used. A household is classified as *poor* if its (per-adult-equivalent) consumption is less than the total poverty line—that is, its total resources are not enough to meet all its basic needs. A household is classified as *food poor* if its (per-adult-equivalent) food consumption is less than the food poverty line—that is, its food consumption does not provide sufficient calories. A household is classified as *extremely poor* if its (per-adult-equivalent) total consumption is less than the food poverty line—that is, its total resources are not enough to meet its basic food needs.

Three poverty measures from the class proposed by Foster, Greer, and Thorbecke (1984) are used to aggregate household-level poverty status to the overall level of poverty in the country: The *poverty incidence* is the percent of the population living in poor households. The *poverty gap* measures how far, on average, the poor population is from the total poverty line. *Poverty severity* not only measures how far the members of the poor population are from the poverty line but also measures inequality among poor households.

The methodology used to estimate poverty in 2018 improves on and therefore diverges from that used in 2003–04 and 2011 (Stats SL and World Bank 2019). In particular, it includes more nonfood items in the aggregate, uses a more appropriate recall period for some items, and adjusts for differences in food prices between rural and urban areas. After construction of the main aggregates and poverty analysis for 2018, comparable measures of poverty between 2003–04, 2011, and 2018 are created and analyzed (for details, refer to the discussion in online appendix A under Trends Methodology).[2]

RESULTS

Poverty and inequality in 2018

Poverty in Sierra Leone remains high. The most recent household survey in Sierra Leone, the 2018 SLIHS, estimates the incidence of poverty at the national poverty line of Le 3,921,000 per adult equivalent annually[3] to be 56.8 percent. Analysis of the 2018 SLIHS also produces a food poverty line of Le 2,125,000 per adult equivalent annually, which results in an extreme poverty rate of 12.9 percent (refer to Stats SL and World Bank 2019, 2020).

Geographic distribution of poverty

Poverty in Sierra Leone is highly concentrated in rural areas, although differences in food poverty are much less pronounced (refer to figure 2.1). Poverty rates in rural areas are more than twice as high as those in urban areas (73.9 percent versus 34.8 percent), and the disparity is even wider for extreme poverty rates (19.9 percent versus 3.8 percent). Rural dwellers account for 56.4 percent of the population but for 73.3 percent of the poor and 87.2 percent of the extremely poor. A marked difference also exists between urban parts of Western Area (the capital city Freetown and outlying towns) and other urban areas: both the poverty rate and the extreme poverty rate are much lower in Western Area Urban, than in other urban areas (22.8 percent versus 49.3 percent and 2.1 percent versus 5.7 percent, respectively). The differences in food poverty are much less pronounced. Although food poverty is higher in rural areas than in urban areas, the difference is much smaller (59.5 percent versus 48.0 percent), and there is little difference between rural areas and urban areas outside of Western Area (59.5 percent versus 57.1 percent). This finding implies that those in rural areas are much poorer overall but are no worse off than urban dwellers (outside of the Western Area) in terms of food consumption.

Poverty rates vary across provinces, with the three poorest districts (Pujehun, Tonkolili, and Falaba) spanning the far south, center, and far northeast of the country. Overall the Northern Province is the poorest (in terms of both total poverty and extreme poverty), and the North West is the least poor

FIGURE 2.1

Poverty rates and numbers, by place of residence

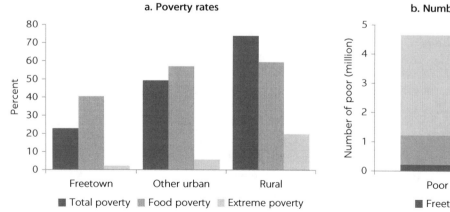
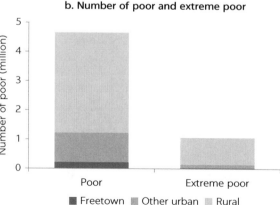

Source: Original calculations using data from the Sierra Leone Integrated Household Survey, 2018.

outside of Western Area. The provincial rates hide significant variation, and the three poorest districts are in both the Northern and Southern Provinces. The least poor districts (outside of Western Area) are Kambia (North West Province), Bonthe (Southern), and Kono (Eastern) (refer to maps A.1 and A.2 in online appendix A). Refer to tables A.2–A.5 in online appendix A for complete poverty rates with standard errors by province and district. Measures of poverty gap and poverty severity show much the same patterns.

Poverty rates for different types of households

Education and sector of employment are the largest predictors of poverty status, but demographic characteristics are also important. The authors consider poverty rates for households based on demographic characteristics, educational achievement and main occupation of the household head, and economic diversification (refer to table A.6 in online appendix A).

Poverty rates are significantly higher for larger households: a household with eight or more members is more than four times as likely to be poor as one with three or fewer members. These larger households represent less than 25 percent of the households in Sierra Leone, but they contain over 40 percent of the population. Households headed by women are somewhat less likely to be poor than those headed by men. Looking at the age of the household head, in general, the older the head, the more likely the household is to be poor.

Moving from demographics to education and employment, strong decreases in poverty with increased education are found. In particular, households whose head finished secondary school are about half as likely to be poor as those whose heads have only a primary school education. By occupation, the poorest households are those whose head is engaged in agriculture. The second most common occupation among household heads in the sample is trading; these households are significantly less poor (42.3 percent) than households whose heads are engaged in agriculture (74.9 percent), but they still have a higher poverty rate than many other occupational groups.

Considering economic activities, the strongest predictor of being poor is working at all in agriculture. Households that engage in some kind of business activities in addition to farming are only slightly less poor than those that rely on farming alone. Those that rely solely on business activities do almost as well as households with at least one member in wage employment.

The highest poverty rates tend to be for the group with the largest share of the population: large households with uneducated heads who engage primarily in agriculture. Households that break this mold one way or another are significantly less likely to be poor.

These various factors are, of course, correlated to each other, Nonetheless, when running a regression analysis on the probability of being poor, most of these factors are still highly significant when controlling for them simultaneously. The results of this regression are presented in table A.7 in online appendix A.

Comparisons to other countries

Based on the international standard of US$1.90 per capita per day (2011 purchasing power parity), the poverty rate in Sierra Leone is 40.7 percent, just above the average for Sub-Saharan Africa (refer to figure A.1 in online appendix A). Note that this rate is significantly lower than the poverty rate with the national poverty line, 56.8 percent, because the national line is higher than the international standard line.

Inequality

Inequality is moderately high in Sierra Leone, with the bottom 40 percent of the population having less than 20 percent of the total household consumption. The top 10 percent of the population has 29.2 percent of the total consumption. Looking at consumption deciles within areas (Western Area Urban, other urban, and rural areas), the patterns are quite similar with less intra-area inequality: within each area the bottom 40 percent has between 30 and 34 percent of total consumption, whereas the top 10 percent has about 15–16 percent of total consumption (refer to figure A.2 in online appendix A).

Inequality, as measured by the Gini coefficient, was 0.357 for Sierra Leone in 2018.[4] This figure varies from 0.348 in Western Area Urban to 0.302 in other urban areas to 0.269 in rural areas. By province, the highest Gini coefficient is found in Western Area Urban, (0.352) followed by the Eastern Province (0.312), and the lowest is the North West Province (0.241).

Growth, poverty, inequality, and shared prosperity, 2003–18

Growth and poverty, 2003–18

Sierra Leone experienced slow but steady growth in the postwar years from 2003 to 2011, which resulted in a significant decrease in poverty. The first SLIHS in 2003 started data collection less than a year after the official end of a devastating 11-year civil war during which the economy contracted significantly[5] and which itself followed a period of stagnation after independence in 1961. The SLIHS found a bleak situation, with two-thirds of the country in poverty and almost one-third of people in extreme poverty unable to meet even their basic food needs. The following years were politically and economically stable, allowing Sierra Leoneans to return to their farms and their businesses and international aid to flow into the country for rebuilding efforts. Per capita GDP grew at an annual average rate of 2.4 percent between 2003 and 2011. Poverty decreased significantly between 2003 and 2011, from 66.4 percent to 53.5 percent.[6] Extreme poverty also decreased significantly, from 31.3 percent to 13.8 percent, as normal economic life returned (refer to figure 2.2).

The years from 2011 to 2018 were more turbulent and saw a more modest reduction in poverty (figure 2.2). Per capita GDP growth accelerated to double-digit rates in 2012 and 2013, largely because of increased iron ore production. This growth was followed by the twin shocks of the Ebola outbreak in 2014 and the fall in international iron prices, which resulted in iron ore operations ceasing production. Iron production declined by 84 percent in 2014 and growth in the rest of the economy slowed to near zero, which led the economy to contract over 20 percent between 2014 and 2016. Since then, the economy has stabilized; it grew slowly and steadily between 2016 and 2018, averaging 2.3 percent per year growth in GDP per capita. The authors analyze poverty between 2011 and 2018 both using the original poverty line calculated in 2003 and constructing a new poverty line for 2018 (for details, refer to the discussion in online appendix A under Trends Methodology). Although the levels of poverty under the two lines are quite different, they both show a modest decrease in total poverty between 2011 and 2018 of 4 to 6 percentage points, and little or no significant change in extreme poverty. Using the 2018 line, poverty decreases from 62.4 percent to 56.8 percent (a 5.6-percentage-point decrease) and extreme poverty increases from 14.4 percent to 15.1 percent (no significant change).

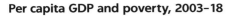

FIGURE 2.2

Per capita GDP and poverty, 2003–18

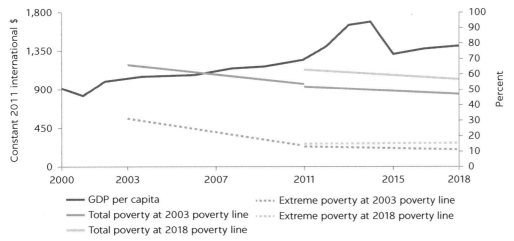

— GDP per capita
— Total poverty at 2003 poverty line
— Total poverty at 2018 poverty line
······ Extreme poverty at 2003 poverty line
······ Extreme poverty at 2018 poverty line

Source: Gross domestic product (GDP) from World Bank World Development Indicators; poverty rates calculated using data from the Sierra Leone Integrated Household Survey, 2003, 2011, and 2018.
Note: The break in the light blue lines at 2011 is due to a slightly different method of adjusting for spatial price differences.

Large reductions in rural poverty between 2003 and 2011 were not repeated between 2011 and 2018. Rural poverty decreased by 12.4 percentage points between 2003 and 2011 but did not change significantly between 2011 and 2018. The trend in extreme poverty is even more stark: a 21.5-percentage-point decrease between 2003 and 2011, followed by a 4.5-percentage-point increase between 2011 and 2018. Urban areas outside of Western Area showed large declines in poverty between 2003 and 2011 and much smaller declines between 2011 and 2018 (refer to figure A.3 in online appendix A).[7]

Changes in poverty since 2011

Although total poverty has decreased nationally, food and extreme poverty have increased, and total poverty has stayed unchanged in rural areas. Using best estimates,[8] poverty decreased by 5.6 percentage points between 2011 and 2018, a significant decrease, although much smaller than the reduction seen in the postwar period between 2003 and 2011. To look more carefully at changes in rural versus urban poverty between 2011 and 2018, a consistent definition of urban across the years is used. Using the 2015 census (which happened approximately halfway between the 2011 and 2018 surveys), geographical boundaries of urban areas for greater Freetown[9] and 15 other major urban centers[10] were identified and each cluster from 2011 and 2018 was classified as being in greater Freetown, other urban centers, or small towns and rural areas. The reduction in total poverty is driven mainly by urban areas: poverty in greater Freetown decreased by 5.8 percentage points and in other urban centers by 7.4 percentage points. Rural areas/small towns have a much smaller, statistically insignificant decrease. Of the four regions, only Western Area has a statistically significant change in poverty (decrease of 7.6 percentage points). Extreme poverty is unchanged overall but decreased in other urban centers (2.7 percentage points) and increased in small towns and rural areas (3.4 percentage points) and in the Eastern Province (5.9 percentage points). Food poverty increased dramatically, by 8.4 percentage points (with double-digit increases in small towns/rural areas, the Northern[11] and Eastern Provinces). Refer to figure A.4 in online appendix A for details. This increase occurred because food consumption as a share of total expenditure[12] decreased from 67 percent to 60 percent, even while food price inflation (in the consumer price index) outpaced nonfood inflation (103 percent versus 84 percent between 2011 and 2018).

The combination of rapid population growth and modest poverty reduction means the number of poor people in Sierra Leone increased between 2011 and 2018. The total number of poor in Sierra Leone increased from an estimated 3.7 million in 2011 to 4.7 million in 2018, and the number of extreme poor increased from 0.8 million to 1.2 million. These increases are mostly concentrated in small towns and rural areas; the number of such poor increased from 3.1 million in 2011 to 3.9 million in 2018 (refer to figure A.5 in online appendix A).

Comparisons to other countries

Sierra Leone falls slightly below the trend in Sub-Saharan Africa for poverty reduction as compared with per capita GDP growth. Using the international standard of US$1.90 per capita per day (in 2011 purchasing power parity) and the welfare measure that is comparable between 2011 and 2018,[13] the poverty rate in Sierra Leone fell slightly, from 50.4 percent in 2011 to 47.2 percent in 2018.[14] The authors graph the reduction (or increase) in poverty using the international line with the mean GDP growth for 20 Sub-Saharan African countries with a survey in 2006–12, and another in 2013–18.[15] Sierra Leone falls in the middle, with average GDP growth and slightly below-average reduction in poverty using this metric (refer to figure A.6 in online appendix A). (Note that a regression analysis on these few countries finds no significant relationship between GDP growth and poverty reduction.) Sierra Leone's growth elasticity of poverty[16] over the period is 0.47. This figure places Sierra Leone in the middle of the distribution for the 20 Sub-Saharan African countries: 10 of the countries have a growth elasticity of poverty between 0.34 and 1.00.

Determinants of poverty reduction

Poverty reduction is the result of a complex interaction of the characteristics of the population and the economic returns to the activities of that population. The working-age population was better educated in 2018 than in 2011; how much does that reduce poverty? Use of contraception has increased since 2011; have smaller household sizes contributed to the reduction in poverty? What about households moving away from relying solely on agriculture? As the population becomes better educated, the premium on education may decrease, resulting in poverty rates creeping up for better-educated households.

Poverty in each year is modeled using a series of binary variables: whether the household is in an urban area, whether it is smaller (fewer than five persons), whether any adult has a secondary or higher education, and whether any adult is working outside of agriculture. All of these variables are highly significant for both years. Simple linear regression is used so that the poverty rate for each year is equal to the predicted value using the population means. *In this regression, the constant can be interpreted as the baseline poverty rate for the most disadvantaged group*. For each variable, the change in poverty that would result (holding everything else constant) from changing the mean value of the variable (from its 2011 value to its 2018 value) and from changing the coefficient on the variable (from the 2011 model to the 2018 model) is considered.[17] In other words, the contribution made by changes in the levels (change in mean value) and returns (change in the coefficient of the variable) of these four variables on poverty is measured.

The biggest contributor to poverty reduction is the strong growth in urban areas, followed by urbanization (more people moving into urban areas). These factors would contribute a 3.6- and a 2.1-percentage-point decrease in poverty, respectively. The baseline poverty rate for the most disadvantaged group has increased 2.2 percentage points. Household sizes have actually gotten slightly larger, which tends to increase poverty. More households have an adult with a secondary education and an adult working in the nonfarm sector, which has contributed to modest reductions in poverty (1.1 and 1.7 percentage points), but these reductions are offset by decreasing coefficients on these variables: having a secondary education or working in a nonfarm sector does not decrease your chance of being poor as much in 2011 as it did in 2018 (refer to table 2.1).

Shared prosperity

The growth rate for the bottom 40 percent between 2011 and 2018 was 9.1 percent, much lower than the rates for the rest of the distribution. By contrast, the rate for the fifth to ninth deciles was 13.7 percent, and the rate for the top 10 percent was 24.2 percent. This pattern is replicated in greater Freetown, which has stronger growth rates across the board. Growth in other urban centers is less strong than in Freetown but is at least pro-poor, with the highest rates for the bottom 40 percent. In small towns and rural areas, there was essentially no growth except for the top 10 percent of the population (refer to figure A.7 in online appendix A).

Growth incidence curves

Growth in Sierra Leone between 2011 and 2018 was not pro-poor. The authors expand on the analysis in the preceding paragraph by looking at the full growth incidence curves. These curves plot real consumption per adult equivalent growth rates against percentiles ranked by consumption per person from poorest to highest and provide a picture of how much growth has favored different population groups.

Figure 2.3 shows the growth incidence curves for Sierra Leone as a whole, for greater Freetown, for other urban centers, and for small towns/rural areas between 2011 and 2018. Growth was almost null in small towns/rural areas for most of the distribution and fairly flat but with slightly higher rates at the very bottom and top ends of the distribution. The authors see again the pro-poor pattern of growth in urban centers outside of Freetown, although the curve displays modest growth rates in the 5–10 percent range for much of the middle of the distribution. Freetown has very high growth rates for the wealthiest households.[18]

TABLE 2.1 **Decomposition of changes in poverty**

| | PERCENT OF HOUSEHOLDS | | COEFFICIENT | | IMPACT ON POVERTY RATE | |
	2011	2018	2011	2018	CHANGE IN MEAN	CHANGE IN COEFF.
Urban	37.03	43.62	−0.2782	−0.3674	−2.13	−3.60
Small household	19.71	18.49	−0.2959	−0.3349	0.38	−0.74
Secondary education	38.67	51.1	−0.0949	−0.0817	−1.1	0.59
Nonfarm work	44.57	65.28	−0.0854	−0.0771	−1.68	0.46
Constant			86.03	88.26		2.23

Source: Original calculations using data from the Sierra Leone Integrated Household Survey, 2011 and 2018.

FIGURE 2.3
Growth incidence curves, by place of residence, 2011–18

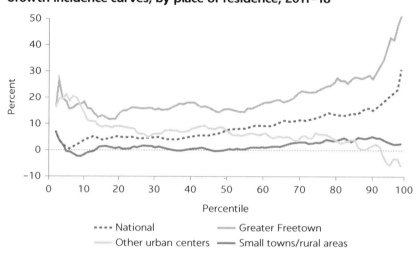

Source: Original calculations using data from the Sierra Leone Integrated Household Survey, 2011 and 2018.

FIGURE 2.4
Share of household consumption, by decile

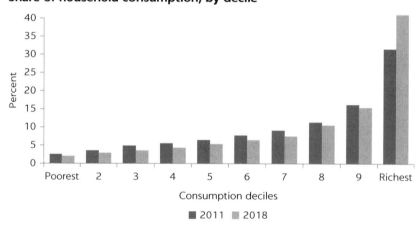

Source: Original calculations using data from the Sierra Leone Integrated Household Survey, 2011 and 2018.

Inequality

Inequality (as measured by the Gini coefficient) increased between 2011 and 2018. Using comparable measures of welfare for 2003 and 2011, the Gini fell from 0.39 to 0.32.[19] Using comparable measures of welfare for 2011 and 2018, the Gini coefficient increased from 0.33 to 0.37.[20] This is the predictable result of a situation in which the areas that are less poor to begin with (urban areas) have higher growth and greater poverty reduction. Figure A.8 in online appendix A shows the Lorenz curves for 2011 and 2018. The authors also look at the share of household consumption by decile and find the same pattern of increasing inequality. All deciles except the richest have a lower share of total household consumption in 2018 than in 2011 (refer to figure 2.4).

The reduction in poverty between 2011 and 2018 in Sierra Leone can also be decomposed into the effect of rising mean levels of welfare (which will tend to reduce poverty), offset by the effect of increasing inequality (which will tend to increase poverty), following the methodology laid out in Datt and Ravallion (1992). This decomposition finds that the contribution due to growth is a 9.0-percentage-point reduction in poverty—that is, poverty would have decreased by 9.0 percentage points had the mean level of income grown at the actual rate between 2011 and 2018 but inequality had remained constant. The increasing inequality contributes a 3.4-percentage-point increase in poverty, so the overall reduction in poverty for Sierra Leone was 5.6 percentage points between 2011 and 2018.

CONCLUSION

Although it is encouraging that Sierra Leone managed a modest poverty reduction over a very turbulent period, the analysis in this chapter also brings out a number of troubling factors as the country seeks to eliminate extreme poverty and achieve middle-income status. The two most important are a failure to reduce extreme poverty and increasing inequality. Extreme poverty actually increased between 2011 and 2018. Although this change is statistically insignificant, extreme poverty increased significantly in certain subsets of the country: small towns and rural areas and the Eastern Province. Combined with high population growth, the total number of poor increased by an estimated 0.4 million between 2011 and 2018. Figure A.9 in online appendix A shows what would happen to poverty rates and numbers by sector if the 2011–18 trends continue for another 20 years. If this pattern of growth continues, extreme poverty will not be eliminated by 2039 and may in fact increase. The country would also become increasingly divided between a prospering urban population and an increasingly deprived rural population; the largest driver in the increase in inequality between 2011 and 2018 was the widening urban-rural gap.

This analysis suggests that, over the 10 years up to 2018, the main driver of poverty reduction was urbanization. Although it is encouraging that poverty rates in urban areas show strong reductions even as the population in these areas swell, there is a limit to relying on urbanization for growth and poverty reduction. Poverty rates are the lowest and growth rates the highest for the capital city, Freetown, but the city is geographically constrained between the mountains and the ocean and is ecologically vulnerable. Deforestation and unplanned expansion have resulted in a catastrophic mud slide in 2017 and annual flooding that takes lives and destroys houses every year. Developing other urban centers outside of Freetown is more promising, especially because they are closer to potentially very valuable mineral resources and agricultural land, but doing so will require addressing unsolved problems in urban planning and land tenure. Analysis of changes in inequality from 2011 to 2018 also shows increased inequality within urban areas; if urbanization outstrips job creation, there is the potential for a growing urban underclass.

Monetary poverty will not be eliminated without addressing rural poverty, particularly that of small-scale subsistence farmers. They are the poorest group, and their poverty rate is increasing. The next chapters in this book set out to determine if, from 2011 to 2018, Sierra Leone made strides in health and education that could lay the foundations for shared prosperity and in addressing long-term poverty in Sierra Leone.

NOTES

1. Statistics Sierra Leone, https://www.statistics.sl/index.php/surveys.html.

2. The online appendixes can be found at https://hdl.handle.net/10986/41206.

3. This comes to about US$1.22 per adult equivalent per day at the average nominal exchange rate for 2018 (Le 8000/US$) or US$2.87 at 2011 purchasing power parity.

4. Based on per capita total household expenditure with population weights.

5. In particular, the capital city was hit by intense fighting in the final years of the war.

6. The rate for 2011 differs slightly from the official one (52.9 percent) because the weights have been adjusted using chiefdom-level growth rates between the 2004 and 2015 censuses.

7. Note that these trends are also influenced by what is considered an "urban" area each year. The analysis uses the classification of EAs as rural or urban that was provided with the data: for 2003 this is the 1985 census; for 2011, the 2004 census; and, for 2018, the 2015 census. A geographically consistent definition of rural versus urban for 2011 and 2018 will also be developed to look at the impact of urbanization on poverty in the next section.

8. Based on the newly calculated 2018 poverty line and comparable welfare indicators for 2011 and 2018.

9. Including Regent, Hastings, Jui, Goderich, Juba, and Adonkia.

10. The five cities with city councils (Kenema, Koidu, Bo, Bonthe, and Makeni) and 10 other major urban areas (Kabala, Mile 91, Waterloo, Magburaka, Port Loko, Lunsar, Kambia, Kamakwie, Kailahun, and Daru).

11. For comparing 2011 to 2018, the definitions of four provinces before the mid-2017 division of the Northern Province into the Northern and North West Provinces are used.

12. For households between the second and seventh deciles.

13. This measure is not as complete as the main aggregate used to analyze poverty in 2018 and does not adjust for differences in prices between rural and urban areas.

14. Note that this figure is higher than the poverty rate given earlier for 2018, because this rate uses the comparable measure of household consumption, which is less complete and therefore lower. This is the weakness of the dollar-a-day standard; it is very sensitive to the coverage of the consumption aggregate. National poverty lines tend to be constructed in such a way that are appropriate to the coverage of the consumption aggregate.

15. Mean GDP growth is taken for the period between the two surveys in each case.

16. That is, the percentage change in poverty divided by the percent change in per capita GDP between 2011 and 2018.

17. It matters which is changed first, so it is done both ways and the average is taken; this is known as the Shapely value. This method is based on Huppi and Ravallion (1991).

18. This result may reflect a real phenomenon, or it may reflect a better response rate among richer households in Freetown or differences in how "outliers" were identified and dealt with. The 2018 data-entry process was more robust, allowing for a much lighter approach to cleaning the data to be taken.

19. Using per capita real consumption and population weights.

20. The Gini coefficient for 2018 presented earlier is slightly lower (0.36), because it is based on a welfare measure that accounts for urban versus rural food prices, which is not possible to do for 2011 or before.

REFERENCES

Datt, G., and M. Ravallion. 1992. "Growth and Redistribution Components of Changes in Poverty Measures: A Decomposition with Applications to Brazil and India in the 1980s." *Journal of Development Economics* 38 (2): 275–95.

Foster, J., J. Greer, and E. Thorbecke. 1984. "A Class of Decomposable Poverty Measures." *Econometrica* 52 (3): 761–6.

Huppi, M., and M. Ravallion. 1991. "Measuring Changes in Poverty: A Methodological Case Study of Indonesia during an Adjustment Period." *World Bank Economic Review* 5 (1): 57–82.

Stats SL (Statistics Sierra Leone) and World Bank. 2019. "Methodology for Consumption-Poverty Estimation, 2018 and Poverty Trends, 2011–2018, in Sierra Leone." Stats SL and World Bank, Freetown, Sierra Leone. https://www.statistics.sl/images/StatisticsSL /Documents/SLIHS2018/SLIHS_2018_New/SLIHS_2018_Methodology_Note_for _Poverty_Calculations.pdf.

Stats SL (Statistics Sierra Leone) and World Bank. 2020. "Poverty and Shared Prosperity in Sierra Leone." World Bank, Washington, DC.

3 Health and Equity

ALEJANDRO DE LA FUENTE AND ELIZABETH M. FOSTER

INTRODUCTION

As noted in chapter 1, the formation of human capital is an unfolding and cumulative process. Proper health care as a newborn and healthy growth in the first years of life are fundamental. Such sequential formation of human capital justifies looking first at mortality and nutritional aspects in children under five before these aspects reverberate into the further processes of human capital accumulation if not addressed properly and in a timely manner.

It was also emphasized that Sierra Leone performs very poorly on the World Bank's Human Capital Index, ranking 151 out of the 157 countries for which the index was calculated.[1] Despite its low ranking, Sierra Leone has made substantial progress on multiple health-related indicators since the end of the war almost 20 years ago. Although 2018 was the first year the Human Capital Index was formally calculated, data on several of the health components (child mortality and stunting) have been collected for a number of years on the Multi-Indicator Cluster Survey (MICS). These surveys have shown progress over time on these indicators. MICS found that, between 2005 and 2017, under-five mortality reduced from 267 deaths per 1,000 live births to 94 per 1,000, while stunting decreased from 40 percent to 26 percent. Maternal mortality (an important component of adult mortality) is harder to estimate, but the best estimates (WHO 2015) suggest a substantial decline, from 1,990 deaths per 100,000 live births in 2005 to 1,360 in 2015, although Sierra Leone's rate remains the highest in the world in this set of estimates (refer to figure 3.1).

Overall national improvements, however, can mask substantial subnational variation, based on either geography or the socioeconomic status of the household, as reflected by monetary welfare or mother's education. Is the progress made overall shared among all the different groups? Is there any sign of a reduction in existing inequalities? If there is, is it due to the bottom of the distribution catching up to the middle or to the middle catching up to the top? Answering these questions will help us understand which groups are being left out and why, enabling continued progress in coming years.

To answer these questions, this chapter looks at the evolution of equity in some key health-related human capital indicators along four dimensions: urban

FIGURE 3.1

Trends in selected health-related indicators, 2005, 2010, and 2017

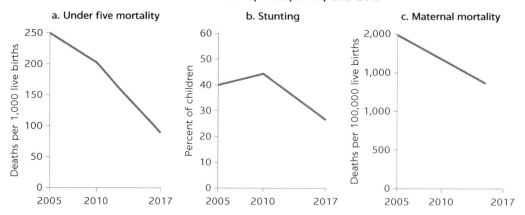

Sources: Original calculations using data from Stats SL 2018; Stats SL and UNICEF-Sierra Leone 2007, 2011; Sierra Leone Integrated Household Survey, 2003, 2011, 2018.

versus rural, welfare quintiles, mother's education, and sex of the child. The authors have microdata from three comparable household surveys over a 12- to 15-year time span for two human capital indicators (under-five mortality and stunting[2]) and one closely related outcome indicator (infant mortality). For each of these indicators, the authors consider the trends for various subgroups based on the sex of the child, area of residence (rural versus urban, sometimes separating urban parts of Western Area from others[3]), welfare quintile (based on either the MICS household wealth index or the Sierra Leone Integrated Household Survey [SLIHS] consumption aggregate), and mother's level of education.

Having identified the trends in these indicators, and their convergence or lack thereof, the authors seek to understand why this is the case. The government of Sierra Leone has really focused on improving maternal and child health and nutrition and encouraging the population to make use of essential services such as seeking antenatal care, coming to health facilities, and bringing children for vaccinations. Have these services been taken up by all segments of the population? Supported by various development partners, the number of clinics in Sierra Leone has almost doubled since the end of the war,[4] and more have been rehabilitated, reaching a high density of coverage. How much has physical access to clinics improved, especially for the poorest and most rural households? Out-of-pocket expenditures for health care, even if low in absolute terms, can be a barrier to access for poor households. In 2010, the Free Health Care Initiative abolished user fees for pregnant women, lactating mothers, and children under the age of five.

The rest of this chapter is organized as follows: The second section describes the data and provides some methodological considerations. The third section presents the trends in selected health outcomes for the various subgroups and then works backward to attempt to understand the patterns described above. The last section presents conclusions.

DATA AND METHODOLOGY

This chapter relies on two main sets of household surveys, the MICS and the SLIHS. Data are available from three rounds of the MICS, conducted by Statistics Sierra Leone and the United Nations Children's Fund in 2005, 2010, and 2017,[5] and the authors use the information on mortality rates, stunting, and use of maternal and child health services. Data are also available for three rounds of the SLIHS, conducted by Statistics Sierra Leone and the World Bank in 2003, 2011, and 2018. These data are used to analyze costs for health services and self-reported time to reach a clinic. All of these surveys are large, nationally representative surveys covering between 3,700 and 8,000 households.

The calculation of mortality rates from household data relies on reports from mothers about all the children they have ever delivered and their survival in order to estimate age-specific exposure and mortality. For 2005 and 2010, under-five mortality was calculated using aggregate data provided by each woman interviewed about how many children she had ever given birth to and how many were still alive. The age of the mother is then used as a proxy for the age of the children and thus their years of exposure. Calculating mortality in this way requires a number of assumptions about the underlying demographics. In 2017, more detailed information was collected, in the form of a complete birth history for each woman, giving the date of birth of each child ever born to the woman and age at death if the child was not still alive. Because of the challenges in replicating the analysis, the figures and results discussed in the next section are based on the reported rates for various subgroups as available in the published reports for each round of the MICS.

Each round of the MICS collected anthropometric data (weight and height or length) on children under the age of five and includes height-for-age Z-scores in the data sets. A child is considered stunted if their height-for-age is less than two standard deviations below the median for a child of that age in months, using World Health Organization standards.[6] Data on vaccinations were also collected at the child level. The type of data collected varies slightly from year to year (and the official government recommendations on under-five vaccinations changed over this period). The exact definition of "vaccination status" constructed was not based on medical recommendations or government policy, but rather on what can be consistently constructed from the available data. Refer to online appendix B and tables B.1–B.5 for details on the estimation of vaccination coverage.[7]

Data on antenatal care, assisted delivery, early childbearing, and contraceptive use were collected on the women's questionnaire of the MICS, administered to women between the ages of 15 and 49. The authors consider whether women who gave birth in the past two years (past five years for 2017) received adequate antenatal care, defined as at least one antenatal care visit from a skilled health care provider (doctor, nurse, midwife, auxiliary nurse, or maternal and child health aide), at least one dose of tetanus vaccine, a blood pressure check, and urine testing.[8] Data on assisted delivery are also based on women who gave birth in the past two years and whether they report that they were attended by a skilled provider. For early childbearing, the authors look at the percent of young women ages 15–19 who have ever given birth and then consider the percent of women (married or in an informal union) who are using a modern form of contraception (that is, female sterilization, male sterilization, pill, intrauterine device, injections, implants, condom, female condom, diaphragm, or foam/jelly).

Data on physical access to clinics and hospitals come from the 2011 and 2018 rounds of the SLIHS and are based on self-reported time to the nearest facility of various types, at the household level. A household is considered to have access to a clinic if the clinic is within 30 minutes and to a hospital if the hospital is within 45 minutes.

Equity in service use and outcomes is considered along three or four dimensions. The first is urban versus rural. For consideration of mortality rate, the authors rely on reported rates, which are given just for urban and rural areas, based on the census designation of the enumeration area in which the household is located.[9] For other indicators, the authors also distinguish between households in urban areas in Western Area and those in the rest of the country. Western Area is the smallest geographically and comprises mainly the capital city, Freetown, and urban areas contiguous with it.

The next dimension is welfare quintile. For analysis using the MICS data, the authors use the wealth quintile constructed by the MICS team. A wealth index is constructed for each household using a principal-components analysis on variables relating mainly to ownership of various household goods, dwelling characteristics, water, and sanitation.[10] This index is then used to divide all households into quintiles. For analysis using the SLIHS, quintiles based on real per-adult-equivalent household consumption-expenditure are used.[11] These two measures are not completely comparable. The MICS wealth index is designed to be a measure of long-term household wealth, whereas the SLIHS welfare measure is based on consumption for one year.

The third dimension is the education level of the woman/child's mother. For mortality, when the authors rely on the previously available figures, education level is broken into three categories: none, primary, and secondary. Because only about 15 percent of women have a secondary education, this level is combined with primary education for other indicators, and women with no education are compared against women with some education.

Finally, for mortality rates, stunting, and vaccination outcomes, the authors consider the sex of the child. For the other outcomes, either there is no child (contraception) or the outcome is determined before the sex of the child is known (early childbearing, antenatal care, assisted delivery, and physical access).

The evolution of each indicator along each dimension over the three rounds of the survey, spanning seven years, is plotted. This method allows consideration of whether improvements in the outcomes have been shared across all groups and whether outcomes are converging or diverging.

Data on health care expenses come from the 2018 round of the SLIHS. Data on health care expenses were collected in several sections of that questionnaire. For each individual in the household, the health section collected data on whether that person was sick or injured or sought medical care for any reason in the past four weeks and, if so, what was paid by the household for the individual's care. It also asked about spending on hospitalization over the past 12 months. These individual-level data also allow us to separate out health care costs for children under five and for women who gave birth in the past year (as a proxy for lactating mothers). Additional information on health care costs is included in the section on vaccinations, which asks about the amount paid for the last vaccination received by each child, and the reproductive health section, which asks about the amount paid at the first antenatal care visit.

RESULTS

Under-five and infant mortality

Under-five and infant mortality rates appear to have converged for various groups. The rates have both declined dramatically since 2005 (from 267 and 158 deaths, respectively, per 1,000 live births in 2005 to 94 and 56 in 2017); and differences based on household wealth, mother's education, and rural/urban appear to have decreased and then disappeared (refer to figures B.1 and B.2 in online appendix B).[12] Most striking is the disappearance of the differences between mortality rates in urban and rural areas and by mother's education. In 2005, infant and under-five mortality rates were about 30 percent higher in rural areas than in urban areas. By 2010, the additional mortality in rural areas was less than 10 percent, and by 2017 mortality rates were actually slightly lower in rural areas. Differences in mortality rates between children of mothers with no education and those of mothers with primary education disappeared between 2005 and 2010, and the difference between them and children of women with secondary education disappeared by 2017.

Differences in mortality rates between richer and poorer houses, or between boys and girls, were never as large, but even those seem to have decreased. Mortality rates for boys were slightly higher than those for girls throughout. Under-five mortality rates for the poorest 60 percent of the population were 13 percent higher than those for the top 40 in 2005; this difference disappeared completely by 2017. For 2010 and 2017, mortality rates by quintile are available. For 2010, there is a clear gradient, with the bottom three quintiles all having rates between 132 and 137 and the top two having rates of 117 and 110. By 2017, there is no gradient: the highest mortality rate is found for the fourth-richest quintile and the lowest rate for the middle quintile.

Stunting

Stunting rates for various groups decreased roughly equally between 2005 and 2017; the only significant difference is seen by wealth quintile. Overall, stunting rates increased slightly between 2005 and 2010, from 40 percent overall to 44 percent, before falling in 2017 to 26 percent. In general, stunting rates for different groups declined in parallel, but there are a couple of noteworthy trends. In 2005, the stunting rates for the bottom 80 percent of the population were statistically indistinguishable, with only the top 20 percent faring better. In 2017, the bottom 60 percent had similar rates, whereas the top 40 percent did better. The gap between children of mothers with no education and those of mothers with some shrank to become statistically insignificant. No substantial gap was seen between girls and boys, although stunting rates were significantly higher (in the statistical sense) for boys in 2010 and for girls in 2017 (refer to figure B.3 in online appendix B).

Key maternal and child health services

The authors next consider three key maternal and child services whose use is likely to influence the child mortality trends described previously: skilled antenatal care, skilled attendance at delivery, and childhood vaccinations. Screening and treatment for prenatal conditions such as high blood pressure, gestational diabetes, and malaria can prevent these conditions from adversely affecting the development of the fetus and can also reduce the risk of maternal mortality. Skilled attendance at delivery should likewise reduce maternal mortality and, thus, neonatal mortality. Childhood vaccinations prevent a wide range of otherwise common diseases that can hamper the physical and cognitive development of a child and even lead to their death.

In addition to antenatal care and assisted delivery, the authors consider two other indicators that are likely to influence maternal mortality: early childbearing and contraceptive use—that is, the percent of young women ages 15–19 who have ever given birth and the percent of women (married or in an informal union) who are using a modern form of contraception. Childbearing early in life carries a significant risk. Use of contraception can help women plan their childbearing and reduce the number of unwanted pregnancies that are too early or too late or follow too closely on a previous birth, all of which are risk factors for maternal mortality.

Rates of antenatal care (as defined in the data and methodology section) have increased significantly and converged strongly. Overall, rates increased from 23 percent in 2005 to 82 percent in 2017. Areas outside of urban areas in the Western Area have caught up, and the difference by welfare quintile has shrunk dramatically. The gap between women with a secondary school education and those without has also decreased (refer to figure B.4 in online appendix B).

Rates of assisted delivery have increased significantly since 2005 and have converged for different groups, with poorer, less-educated, and rural women catching up to others. Overall, the rate of assisted delivery almost doubled between 2005 and 2017, increasing from 43 percent to 82 percent. Gains were concentrated in women in the poorest 80 percent of households who have been catching up to the richest 20 percent. The gap between educated and uneducated women has also narrowed, and the gap between rural and urban women has narrowed significantly; coverage for rural women has more than doubled, from 35 percent to 77 percent. Also, after an initial decline in coverage, rates of antenatal care in urban areas outside Western Area have increased to surpass those within it (refer to figure B.5 in online appendix B).

Rates of childhood vaccinations have converged slightly, looking at household wealth and mother's education. There were never large differences in childhood vaccination rates between households of different wealth levels. Childhood vaccination rates have actually fallen slightly in urban parts of Western Area. The authors consider whether children ages 12–23 months have received four vaccinations: at least one dose of measles; at least one dose of bacille Calmette-Guérin; at least one dose of diphtheria, pertussis, tetanus (whether separately or as part of the pentavalent vaccination schedule); and at least three doses of oral polio vaccine.[13] Rural households actually have slightly higher rates of vaccination coverage as of 2017. Childhood vaccination rates are below 80 percent for every subgroup, even the richest quintile of households (refer to figure B.6 in online appendix B). Looking at the data on vaccinations for 2017 in more detail, significant differences in vaccination rates by region are evident: 84 percent in the east and 85 percent in the south versus 69 percent in the north and 68 percent in the west.[14] Vaccination rates are also higher for children who receive some kind of registration at birth or soon after: vaccination rates are only 34 percent for children who never received an under-five card and 58 percent for those whose birth was never registered.

Use of modern contraception has increased from negligible levels in 2005 but remains low and shows limited convergence between different groups.

Overall, the use of a modern form of contraception has increased from only 4 percent to 21 percent. These gains are pretty evenly spread across different groups of women, although urban areas outside of the Western Area caught up to other urban areas, and the fourth quintile caught up to the top quintile (refer to figure B.7 in online appendix B).

Rates of early childbearing have declined only slightly; the biggest reductions are seen for young women with no education, whose rates decline to be much closer to those of better-educated young women.[15] Looking at the percent of women ages 15–19 who have ever given birth, there are declines from 31 percent in 2005 to 19 percent in 2017. In all years, the rates are significantly lower for the richest quintile but indistinguishable among the bottom 80 percent of the population. Rates for young women with some education have stayed basically unchanged, whereas those for young women with no education have decreased from 46 percent to 30 percent (refer to figure B.8 in online appendix B).

Physical access to clinics and hospitals

The fraction of households with a clinic within 30 minutes by their usual form of transportation increased from 22 percent in 2011 to 57 percent in 2018. The improvements were basically identical across welfare quintiles and between urban and rural areas, with no signs of disadvantaged households catching up but also no signs of the gap widening. Unlike for some other indicators, there is no difference between urban areas in the Western Area and those elsewhere in terms of physical access to clinics (refer to figure B.9 in online appendix B).

Reported access to hospitals (percent of households with a hospital within 45 minutes) remained constant at about 60 percent of households between 2011 and 2018.[16] Interestingly, there is some divergence in rates by quintile and urban/rural (refer to figure B.10 in online appendix B). This disparity may be due to the increasing inequality and concentration of the poor in rural areas (Stats SL and World Bank 2020). The widening gap between rural and urban areas may also be due to the reclassification of areas in the 2015 census: many larger rural communities (likely closer to a hospital) were reclassified as urban in the 2015 census, which especially affected communities in Western Area Rural.

Cost of health care services

Even if households have physical access to a clinic, they may still fail to make use of important maternal and child health services because of the cost of these services. Costs for antenatal care, childhood vaccinations, and treatment of sick children are considered. Failure to access treatment for sick children increases the likelihood that they will die of easily treatable conditions such as malaria and diarrheal diseases, as well as the likelihood that, even if they survive, their growth will be stunted and their development impaired.

Despite the Free Health Care Initiative, most women report paying for antenatal care. Vaccinations are almost always provided for free. Most women access antenatal care at either a government hospital (25 percent) or a government clinic (69 percent). Of these women, 59 percent and 67 percent, respectively, paid for antenatal care (refer to figure 3.2). The amounts paid were generally low—the median amount paid on the first antenatal care visit was Le 15,000 (less than US$2) at government hospitals and Le 10,000 at government clinics. In contrast, vaccinations are usually provided free.[17] Although most children received their last vaccination either at a government hospital (22 percent) or government clinic (58 percent), a substantial number (16 percent) received it from mobile vaccination teams visiting households. The percent of children whose parents had to pay for childhood vaccinations is only 5 percent, 12 percent, and 2 percent, respectively, for those sources (refer to figure 3.2), and the median amounts are all under US$1.

Households also bear significant expenses for the treatment of sick children under the age of five, despite these services being officially free. Again, government hospitals and clinics are the main sources of treatment for sick children under five, representing 19 percent and 64 percent, respectively, of visits. Most households taking their sick children under five to these facilities, 67 percent and 59 percent, respectively, have to pay. The amounts paid are not trivial for poor households; the respective charges, Le 42,000 (about US$5.00) and Le 20,000 (US$2.35), are comparable to amounts paid by those who sought care for their sick children at pharmacies or private clinics. Note the gradients in probability of paying by household wealth: richer households are more likely to pay for a sick child and less likely to pay for antenatal care, even when restricting the analysis to children seen at government health care facilities (refer to figure 3.3). The largest part of the expenses (wherever treatment is sought) is purchasing medicines from the health care provider (refer to figure B.11 in online appendix B).

Health expenses represent about 6 percent of total household expenditures, but the vast majority of health care costs are not for pregnant women or children under five. Health care spending for children under five and for pregnant women and lactating mothers[18] represents less than 0.5 percent of total household expenditure. Health care costs as a percent of household expenditure rise by household welfare but are slightly higher in rural areas than in urban ones (refer to figure B.12 in online appendix B).

FIGURE 3.2

Fraction of households paying for maternal and child health care services, by place of residence, type of facility, and consumption quintile

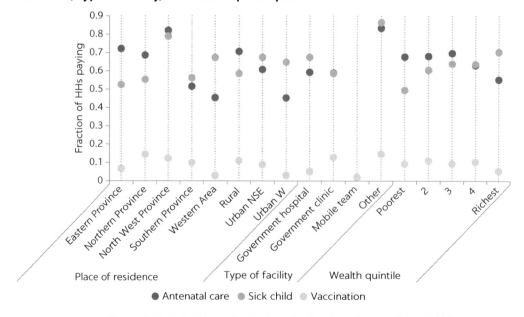

Source: Original calculations using data from the Sierra Leone Integrated Household Survey, 2018.
Note: HH = household; NSE = Northern, Southern, and Eastern Provinces; W = Western Area.

FIGURE 3.3

Distribution of maternal and child health care expenses, by place of residence, type of facility, and consumption quintile

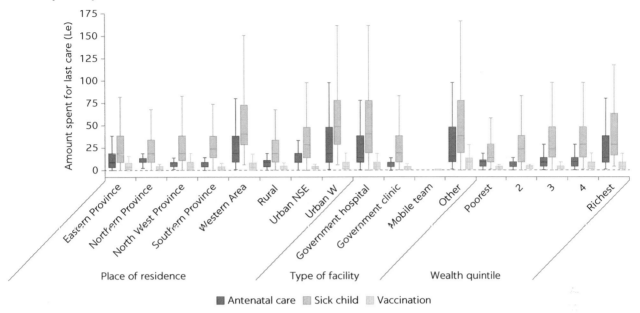

Source: Original calculations using data from the Sierra Leone Integrated Household Survey, 2018.
Note: Le = Sierra Leonean leones; NSE = Northern, Southern, and Eastern Provinces; W = Western Area.

CONCLUSION

Under-five and infant mortality rates have seen significant improvements since 2005 and a significant decrease in inequity. The decrease in the rate of stunting has been less dramatic, with less convergence. These improvements are likely due to increased access to clinics and increased use of basic maternal health care and nutrition services. All sectors of the population have benefited from increased access to clinics, and less advantaged groups have joined more advantaged ones in having very high rates of use of basic maternal health services. These improvements also likely explain some of the reduction in maternal mortality, especially for the most disadvantaged. Use of modern contraceptives has increased from almost zero although the rates are still low and little change has been seen in rates of early childbearing. Increases in childhood vaccination rates have not been as strong, and rates for urban parts in the Western Area have actually declined since 2010, perhaps partially explaining why child mortality rates have been stagnant in urban areas over that period. Even though access to clinics has improved, it is still low in rural areas: only 40 percent of households in rural areas have a clinic within 30 minutes. Improving the transportation network and reducing costs could be a more effective way to increase access than building yet more facilities. Households still also bear significant costs for the treatment of sick children under five, despite the Free Health Care Initiative. Removing these barriers may help poor and rural households make better use of antenatal and postnatal care, childhood vaccinations (which requires bringing a child to the clinic many times over the first year of life), and treatment for sick children, which should further decrease mortality and stunting rates.

NOTES

1. This index is based on five indicators: probability of survival to age five, expected years of school, harmonized test scores, children under five not stunted, and adult (ages 15 to 60) survival rates (refer to Kraay 2019).
2. These indicators were selected on the basis of data availability in all three rounds of the MICS used.
3. The western region is by far the smallest and contains the capital city, Freetown, and its suburbs outside the city boundaries. Other urban areas within the Western region are mainly a series of towns between the east of Freetown and the city of Waterloo, forming a continuous urban area.
4. The number of Peripheral Health Units increased from 622 in 2004 to 1,181 in 2017 (MoHS 2004, 2017).
5. An earlier round of the MICS was conducted in 2000 but is not used. There are some data-quality issues, which is understandable given that fieldwork was disrupted by fighting during the closing phase of the war. For more information on the MICS, refer to the following publications: Stats SL (2018) and Stats SL and UNICEF-Sierra Leone (2007, 2011).
6. For 2010 and 2017, the authors were able to replicate exactly the stunting rates presented in the published reports. For 2005, the rates constructed from the microdata tended to be slightly higher than those in the published report. For example, the authors calculate the overall rate of stunting to be 41.6 percent as opposed to the published figure of 40.1 percent.
7. The online appendixes can be found at https://hdl.handle.net/10986/41206.
8. These components are chosen because they are parts of the government of Sierra Leone's package of antenatal care, and data on them are available for every round of the survey.
9. Note that the 2015 census, which occurred between the second and third round of both surveys, remapped the enumeration areas and reclassified them, resulting in many areas that had previously been classified as rural being reclassified as urban.
10. For details on the construction of the wealth index for 2017, refer to footnote 30 to table SR5.1.W in Stats SL (2018).
11. For details on the construction of real per adult equivalent consumption-expenditure, refer to Stats SL and World Bank (2019).
12. As Stats SL (2018) admits, the rates of child mortality it finds are significantly below the trends estimated by other means/surveys. The complete lack of any gradient in child mortality by wealth quintile in 2017 is also somewhat suspicious.
13. These are the key vaccinations for which coverage rates can be constructed in a comparable fashion for all three years, replicating numbers published in the MICS reports. Refer to online appendix B for more details.
14. This low rate in the west is despite the fact that participation in door-to-door vaccination campaigns in generally highest in the Western Area.
15. Note that each generation of young women is better educated that the previous; in 2005, just under half of the women ages 15–19 had ever attended school and, in 2017, 84 percent of them had.
16. This lack of change is consistent with the fact that new hospitals in previously unserved areas have not been opened over this period.
17. Based on anecdotal evidence about when fees are charged, women who were/had been pregnant were asked how much they paid for their first antenatal visit when they registered with the facility for antenatal care. Caregivers of children were asked how much they paid for the last vaccination received by their child, which may miss some costs in clinics collecting a fee to issue the Under Five card on which vaccinations and height/weight are recorded.
18. Outpatient health care costs were asked with a four-week recall period. These expenses were counted as expenses for a pregnant/lactating mother if they were for a woman who had been pregnant or given birth within the past year, even though some of these women could have miscarried earlier in the year or given birth earlier in the year and no longer be breastfeeding. Note that expenses for hospitalization (following general practice) are not included in income aggregates. Costs associated with giving birth were not included on the SLIHS questionnaire and are, therefore, not presented.

REFERENCES

Kraay, A. 2019. "The World Bank Human Capital Index: A Guide." *World Bank Research Observer* 34 (1): 1–33.

MoHS (Sierra Leone, Ministry of Health and Sanitation). 2004. *National Operational Handbook for Primary Health Care*. Freetown: MoHS, Government of Sierra Leone.

MoHS (Sierra Leone, Ministry of Health and Sanitation). 2017. *Summary Report of the 2017 SARA Plus in Sierra Leone*. Freetown: MoHS, Government of Sierra Leone.

Stats SL (Statistics Sierra Leone). 2018. *Sierra Leone Multiple Indicator Cluster Survey 2017*. Survey Findings Report. Freetown: Stats SL.

Stats SL (Statistics Sierra Leone) and UNICEF-Sierra Leone. 2007. *Sierra Leone Multiple Indicator Cluster Survey 2005*. Final Report. Freetown: Statistics Sierra Leone and UNICEF-Sierra Leone.

Stats SL (Statistics Sierra Leone) and UNICEF-Sierra Leone. 2011. *Sierra Leone Multiple Indicator Cluster Survey 2010*. Final Report. Freetown: Statistics Sierra Leone and UNICEF-Sierra Leone.

Stats SL (Statistics Sierra Leone) and World Bank. 2019. "Methodology for Consumption-Poverty Estimation, 2018 and Poverty Trends, 2011–2018, in Sierra Leone." Stats SL and World Bank, Freetown, Sierra Leone. https://www.statistics.sl/images/StatisticsSL /Documents/SLIHS2018/SLIHS_2018_New/SLIHS_2018_Methodology_Note_for _Poverty_Calculations.pdf.

Stats SL (Statistics Sierra Leone) and World Bank. 2020. "Poverty and Shared Prosperity in Sierra Leone." World Bank, Washington, DC.

WHO (World Health Organization). 2015. *Trends in Maternal Mortality: 1990 to 2015: Estimates by WHO, UN ICEF, UN FPA, World Bank Group and the United Nations Population Division*. Geneva: WHO.

4 Education and Equity

ALEJANDRO DE LA FUENTE AND ELIZABETH M. FOSTER

INTRODUCTION

Education is widely considered an essential input for growth and for reducing poverty (Barro 1991; World Bank 2018). The ability to read and write enhances people's ability to secure better jobs later in life and to do those jobs more efficiently. The effect is highest in Sub-Saharan Africa, where, on average, an additional year of schooling leads to about a 13 percent increase in wage earning (Montenegro and Patrinos 2014). Being educated is also a right that enhances people's ability to engage in discussion, to debate, to negotiate, and to add their voice to influence decisions at the household and local levels. Thus, being educated is valuable in itself and can improve the quality of people's lives in ways beyond income-enhancing productivity (Sen 1997). By contrast, lower educational attainment among children is one of the main factors that may perpetuate poverty over a child's life and across generations (Narayan et al. 2018). Proper health and education are central to long-term poverty reduction in Africa.

The quantity and quality of education children receive will greatly contribute to their productivity later in life, in both the economic and the social realms. Inequality in education leads to inequality in economic outcomes for the next generation. Reducing inequalities in education and making sure that every child has the opportunity to complete his or her education are essential for reducing both poverty and inequality.

Sierra Leone has made substantial progress on multiple education indicators since the end of the war almost 20 years ago. Supported by various development partners, the government of Sierra Leone has constructed or rehabilitated a huge number of schools. In 2003, there were only 4,015 primary schools and 246 secondary schools in the entire country (World Bank 2007). By 2018, the number of primary schools had almost doubled to 7,112 primary schools and the number of secondary schools had increased almost 10-fold, to 2,146 (World Bank 2007 and original calculations using data from the 2018 Annual School Census).

Using data from the Sierra Leone Integrated Household Survey (SLIHS), the authors calculate that expected years of schooling increased from 8.5 in 2003 to 9.7 in 2018.[1] The primary completion rate increased from 34.2 percent in 2003 to 66.4 percent in 2018. Gains in gross and net enrollment rates were more modest, especially at the primary education level, but net enrollment rates at the secondary level did increase (refer to figure 4.1). Enrollment rates also dramatically increased, particularly for girls. Gross enrollment rates in primary school increased from 60.4 for girls and 85.3 for boys in 2001 to 114.7 and 110.8, respectively.[2] For secondary school, they increased from 20.3 percent for girls and 28.1 percent for boys to 95.7 and 99.9. These rates are now on par with other countries in Sub-Saharan Africa, and the gender gap is in fact smaller than in the region as a whole, especially at the secondary school level.

As noted in chapter 3, overall national improvements can mask substantial subnational variation, based on either geography or the socioeconomic status of the household, such as monetary welfare or mother's education. Such variation raises the questions of whether different groups all share in the progress, whether existing inequalities are reduced, and what movement among the income distribution accounts for the reduction.

To answer these questions, this chapter looks at the evolution of two education indicators of particular interest—primary completion rates and expected years of schooling—along four dimensions: urban versus rural, welfare quintiles, mother's education, and sex of the child. The authors have microdata from three comparable household surveys over 15 years for expected years of schooling and for primary school completion. For each indicator, the trends for various subgroups are considered based on the sex of the child, area of residence (rural versus urban, sometimes separating urban areas in the Western Area from others[3]), welfare quintile (based on the SLIHS consumption aggregate), and mother's level of education.

FIGURE 4.1

Trends in education indicators, 2003–18

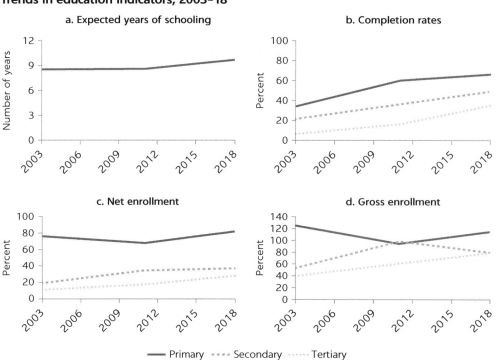

Source: Original calculations using data from the Sierra Leone Integrated Household Survey, 2003, 2011, and 2018.

Having identified the trends in these indicators, and their convergence or lack thereof, the authors seek to understand the reasons for these trends. How much has physical access to schools improved, especially for the poorest and most rural households? Out-of-pocket expenditures for education, even if low in absolute terms, can be a barrier to access for poor households. From September 2018, the Free Quality School Education Program (FQSE) abolished school fees at many public schools.[4] However, even if services are officially free, there may be unofficial costs to be paid or costs for items (for example, school uniforms) not covered under the programs. The authors also consider in more detail the education careers of students. Which children fail to start school or drop out and why?

The rest of this chapter is organized as follows: The second section describes the data and provides some methodological considerations. The third and fourth sections present the trends in selected educational outcomes for the various subgroups and then work backward to attempt to understand the patterns seen as described previously. The fifth section presents conclusions.

DATA AND METHODOLOGY

This chapter relies mainly on the SLIHS, conducted by Statistics Sierra Leone with support from the World Bank in 2003–04, 2011, and 2018.[5] The authors use this information to construct expected years of schooling and primary school completion, as well as to analyze costs for education services and self-reported time to travel to schools. SLIHS data are supplemented by additional data from the Annual School Censuses in 2018 and 2019 and the Population and Housing Census from 2015. Data from those censuses are used to model physical access to schools based on distance, and to define and compare catchment areas for schools that benefit from the FQSE to those for schools that do not receive this benefit.

The main education indicator considered is expected years of schooling. For the World Bank Human Capital Index (HCI), this indicator is defined as the number of years of school that a child can expect to obtain between ages 4 and 18, including preschool. It is ideally calculated from age-specific enrollment rates (Kraay 2019), although this is not always done in practice owing to unavailability of data. For the HCI, it is instead calculated using total net enrollment rates for primary, lower-secondary, and upper-secondary education, as reported by the United Nations Educational, Scientific, and Cultural Organization. For the purposes of this chapter, the expected years of schooling indicator is calculated somewhat differently than is done for the HCI. First, preschool is not considered, because data on preprimary education are not available for 2003 and 2011. (As in the HCI, the SSS4, a fourth year of senior secondary school [SSS] that was introduced and then reversed after just a couple of years, is not included.) Second, the indicator is calculated using age-specific enrollment rates constructed from microdata, rather than one total net enrollment rate by level (primary, junior secondary, and senior secondary). Specifically, for each age from 5 to 17, the authors calculate the fraction of children of that age who are obtaining an additional year of school—that is, are enrolled in school and not repeating the same class as last year. Expected years of schooling is the sum of these fractions, either as calculated for all observations in our data set or a subpopulation that contains all age groups, such as urban students or female students. Refer to online appendix C and table C.1 for more details on the estimation of the expected years of schooling.[6]

The Sierra Leonean school context (many children not in the official class for their age) and data quality (various gaps and biases in age data) make interpreting changes in some education indicators difficult. When large numbers of children are in the incorrect class for their age, changes in gross and net enrollment rates can be difficult to interpret. A primary gross enrollment rate can increase either because more children enter the school system or because children fail to pass exams and progress to secondary school. Because most students of senior secondary age are still in junior secondary school, or JSS (and, in fact, more are still in primary school than have progressed to SSS), small changes in cohort size can also lead to meaningless changes in net or gross enrollment rates. In addition, there are problems with the data on ages. First, the age, even of children, is not always known, which results in rounding and heaping at age 10. Second, there is frequent undercounting of under-fives, which sometimes results in heaping at older ages. Third, even if current age is given correctly, it is not always equal to age at the start of the school year (most six-year-olds in June would have been only five when the current school year started the preceding September). Therefore, in this chapter, the standard education indicators of net enrollment rates and gross enrollment rates are not used. Refer to figure C.1 in online appendix C for details on the reported age distribution in each round of the SLIHS.

The other education outcome indicator that is used is primary school completion. The *primary school completion rate* is the percent of children three to five years older than the intended age for the last grade of primary school (thus, ages 14–16 in Sierra Leone) who have completed that grade. This indicator is less sensitive to the exact ages of children and allows for them to be several years behind the official school schedule. Therefore, it avoids many of the issues that arise with gross and net enrollment rates.

The authors also consider physical access to schools, using two different sources of data. The first is self-reported time to travel to the nearest primary school and nearest secondary school from the 2011 and 2018 rounds of the SLIHS. A household is considered to have access to a primary or secondary school if the nearest school is within 30 minutes travel time of the household.

AN OVERVIEW OF EDUCATION IN SIERRA LEONE

Structure of the education sector

Education in Sierra Leone follows a six-three-three pattern, with external exams determining progress to the next level. Education starts at age six with six years of primary school, after which students sit the National Primary School Examination; then three years of JSS, after which they sit the Basic Education Certificate Examination; then three years of SSS, after which they sit the West Africa Senior Secondary School Certificate Examination.[7] The exams are administered by the West Africa Examination Council. The government has recently started scaling up the provision of public preprimary schools for children ages three to five. There is only one JSS for every five primary schools, and only one SSS for every three JSSs. Preprimary and senior secondary schools are concentrated in urban areas: 45 percent of preprimary schools and 40 percent of

SSSs are in the greater Freetown area, and another 18 percent and 19 percent, respectively, are in other major urban centers.[8]

Education services are provided by a mix of government and nongovernment providers. Over half the schools are "government-assisted" or "mission" schools—that is, schools that were started by various Christian and Muslim mission organizations but are now largely managed by the government and whose teachers are mostly on the government payroll. Smaller numbers of schools are wholly government-run (14 percent) or community schools started by the community but receiving some level of support from the government (14 percent). The remainder of the schools are private schools. The breakdown of schools by level and management is shown in table 4.1.

The government of Sierra Leone supports public schools by paying teachers, providing school materials, and providing block grants to schools. Before the introduction of the FQSE, public primary schools were supposed to receive Le 15,000 per pupil per year (and primary education was supposed to be free, but this requirement was entirely unenforced). Just over half the teachers at government schools and just under half the teachers at mission schools are on the government payroll (teachers on the government payroll are paid directly by the central government; the money does not pass through the schools). As table 4.2 shows, community schools rely heavily on families and the community in general to pay over a third of their teachers. In all types of schools, including private, a substantial number of teachers work for free (about half of these volunteers have no formal qualification).

TABLE 4.1 **Schools and students, by ownership and level**

OWNERSHIP	PREPRIMARY	PRIMARY	JUNIOR SECONDARY	SENIOR SECONDARY	TOTAL
Number of schools					
Community	256	883	347	95	1,581
Government	151	1,164	166	61	1,542
Mission (government-assisted)	722	4,416	784	306	6,228
Private	627	692	333	161	1,813
Total	1,756	7,155	1,630	623	11,164
Percent of schools					
Community	14.6	12.3	21.3	15.3	14.2
Government	8.6	16.3	10.2	9.8	13.8
Mission (government-assisted)	41.1	61.7	48.1	49.1	55.8
Private	35.7	9.7	20.4	25.8	16.2
Total	100	100	100	100	100
Percent of students					
Community	15.7	9.6	19.0	13.1	11.9
Government	10.5	19.1	16.0	18.8	18.1
Mission (government-assisted)	44.7	65.9	57.5	58.8	62.6
Private	29.1	5.4	7.5	9.3	7.4
	100	100	100	100	100

Source: Original calculations using data from Sierra Leone's 2018 Annual School Census.

TABLE 4.2 **Source of teacher salaries, by school ownership**

	COMMUNITY	GOVERNMENT	MISSION (GOVERNMENT-ASSISTED)	PRIVATE
Government payroll	20.6	51.9	43.3	0.8
Families/community	39.1	16.7	17.4	12.1
Private institution	11.8	7.2	12.8	78.9
Volunteer	28.5	24.2	26.6	8.2
	100.0	100.0	100.0	100.0

Source: Original calculations using data from Sierra Leone's 2019 Annual School Census.

RESULTS

The first part of this section presents how primary school completion rate and expected years of schooling changed between 2003 and 2018, with a particular focus on equity. In particular, the authors look at the size of the gap between more and less advantaged groups (by sex, household wealth, location, and mother's education) and whether that gap has been widening or closing. The second part of the section explores some plausible reasons behind the outcomes observed.

Trends in primary completion rate and expected years of schooling

As noted in the introduction, Sierra Leone has made substantial progress since the end of the civil war in 2002 in increasing primary school completion rates and expected years of schooling. But have these gains been shared equally across the population? If not, how big are the inequalities in educational attainment? Groups in the middle of the income distribution, but not the most disadvantaged children, have managed to catch up in primary school completion. Looking at primary school completion by sex, there has not been a significant difference between girls and boys since 2003. The three middle quintiles have gained, pulling away from the lowest quintile and closing the gap with the richest quintile. Similarly, the gap between urban areas in the Western Area and those outside it has narrowed. Considering mother's education, the gap between children whose mother completed at least primary school and those whose mother did not has narrowed slightly but remains wide (refer to figure C.2 in online appendix C).

Moving beyond completing primary school, this chapter looks at the total number of years of schooling a child can expect to achieve. This number is calculated using the age-specific probability that children (of a certain subgroup) are achieving an additional year of schooling (that is, that they are still in school and not just repeating the same class as last year). Combining these probabilities gives the expected years of schooling. These age-specific rates for 2003, 2011, and 2018 are shown in figure C.3 in online appendix C. Note that rates of achieving an additional year of school for younger students (ages five to nine) actually fell between 2003 and 2011. This drop may reflect the normalization of the education sector, after a backlog of students in the early years following the end of the war, or may be an artifact of the data owing to the particularly implausible distribution of ages seen in the 2011 data (refer to figure C.1 in online appendix C). Between 2011 and 2018, there was a clear increase in rates of achieving an additional year for children of all ages.

Overall, expected years of schooling increased from 8.5 in 2003 to 8.6 in 2011 to 9.7 in 2018. Looking at differences across various groups of children, groups in the middle appear to be catching up in terms of expected years of schooling, but the most disadvantaged children do not. A small difference between boys and girls in 2003 closed completely by 2011. The authors also see urban areas outside of the Western Area achieving parity with those in the Western Area by 2018 (refer to figure C.4 in online appendix C).

Challenges to children's school attendance and completion

As noted in the previous section, since the end of civil conflict in the early 2000s, Sierra Leone has experienced gains on key education indicators (expected years of schooling and primary school completion), particularly among households in the middle of the income distribution and in urban areas outside the capital city. This section explores plausible underlying factors that have prevented remote and poor households from catching up with the rest of the population, with particular emphasis on access to schools and school expenses as important barriers to education.

Children born since the end of the war have mostly attended school, with girls doing as well as boys. Most children start school: 88 percent of children ages 6–17 have ever attended school. The rate is actually slightly higher for girls (89 percent) than for boys (87 percent), reversing a large disparity between males and females that exists for all older groups. It is a significant improvement over the previous cohort born during the war: only 76 percent of that cohort, and only 69 percent of girls, ever attended school. Mean years of education is also almost identical for girls and boys up to age 18 or so (refer to figure C.5 in online appendix C).

Children who have never attended school are concentrated in rural areas and the poorest households. Over 20 percent of children in the poorest quintile have never attended school, compared to less than 5 percent in the richest. For rural areas, the figure is 17 percent, compared to less than 4 percent in both greater Freetown and other urban areas (refer to figure C.6 in online appendix C).

Perceived lack of relevance/usefulness of school is the most common reason why children do not attend school, followed by financial reasons. Expense is the most common reason children who start school drop out, followed by marriage and pregnancy for girls (refer to chapter 6). Of children (ages 7–17 at the time of the survey) who never went to school, the reason given for 33 percent of them was that parents did not value school (note that in most cases parents were the respondents for this section) and for 9 percent that the child was not interested (both responses are included under "Interest/ usefulness" in figure 4.2). Expense was cited for 32 percent of children and distance for 14 percent. Considering children/young adults (ages 6–24) who have left school, 54 percent of boys and 34 percent of girls reported that it was because of expense, 36 percent of girls because of pregnancy, and 18 percent of boys and 12 percent of girls because school was useless or uninteresting. These reasons do not vary much by welfare quintile; expense continues to be an issue even for the richest households.

Even though most children enroll in school, they fall behind the appropriate class for their age and few manage to complete their education. Owing to some late starts and high rates of repetition, students fall behind their correct

FIGURE 4.2

Reasons for never starting school and for dropping out, by child's sex and consumption quintile

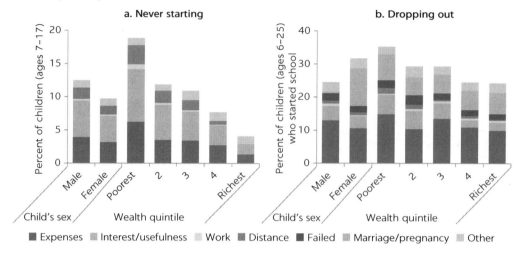

Source: Original calculations using data from the Sierra Leone Integrated Household Survey, 2018.

class for age. Among children of SSS age (15–17) at school, 21 percent are still in primary school and 55 percent in JSS. Young women ages 20–30 have just 6.0 years of education on average, and young men have 8.5 years (refer to figures C.7 and C.8 in online appendix C). Gross enrollment rates are well over 100 percent for primary school (reflecting the fact that many over-age children are still in primary school) but fall off sharply for JSS and SSS. Net enrollment rates follow the same pattern, starting off at 82.1 percent, then falling to only 17.3 percent for SSS. There is little gender gap for students: through JSS, girls' enrollment rates are as high as or higher than those for boys (refer to figure C.9 in online appendix C).

Costs of education services before FQSE

Educational expenses represent a significant burden for poor households, and, as seen in the previous section, are frequently cited as one of the reasons children do not start school or as the main reason they drop out. The authors consider data on education spending from the 2018 SLIHS, which cover the period before the introduction of FQSE.[9] The median annual education cost per student is Le 150,000 (US$18) for primary school, Le 475,000 (US$56) for JSS and Le 700,000 (US$82) for SSS. These amounts are significantly higher for private schools, in the Western Area, and for the richest households (refer to figure 4.3).

School fees represent only about 17 percent of the total cost of education at public schools.[10] This total cost ranges from 15 percent for primary school to 23 percent for SSS. The FQSE program mainly targets eliminating school fees, which will reduce but not eliminate out-of-pocket education expenses for households. The program also provides some textbooks, but schoolbooks of all kinds represent only about 5 percent of the cost. School spending on education is widely spread across a range of categories. Looking at students in public schools, after school fees, the biggest expense is uniforms (11 percent of the total), followed by schoolbags (9 percent). Books, school supplies, and extra classes[11] each account for about 5 percent of the total cost (refer to figure C.10 in online appendix C).

FIGURE 4.3

Distribution of school expenses, by place of residence, type of school, and consumption quintile

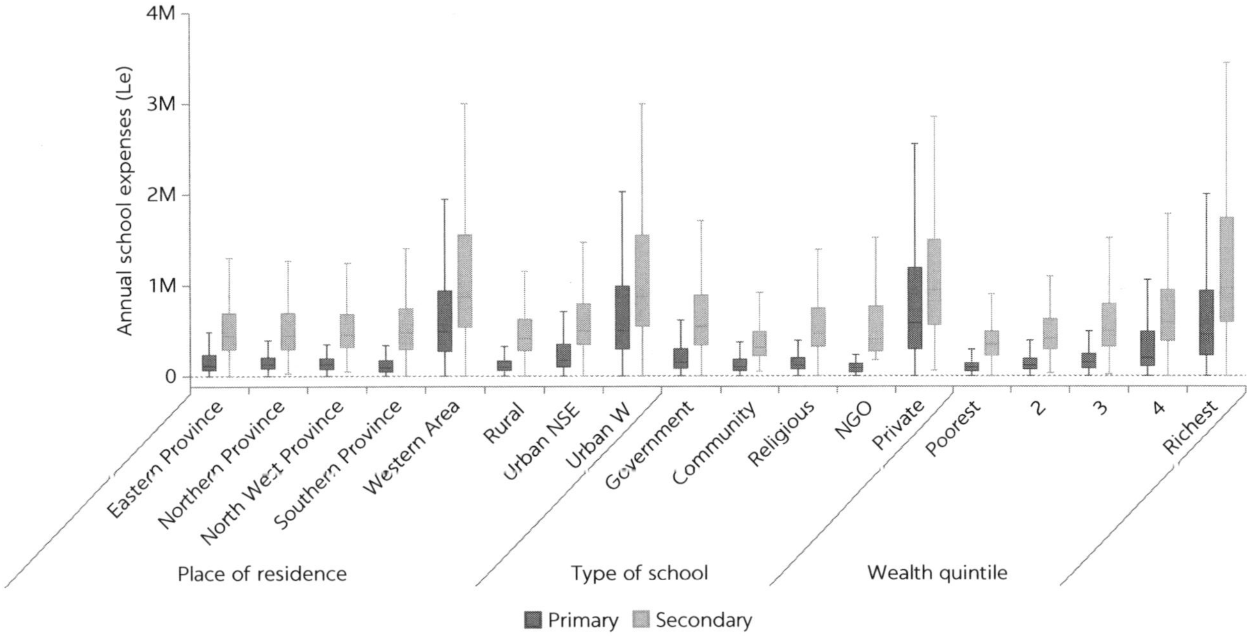

Source: Original calculations using data from the Sierra Leone Integrated Household Survey, 2018.
Note: Le = Sierra Leonean leones; NGO = nongovernmental organization; NSE = Northern, Southern, and Eastern Provinces; W = Western Area.

Education expenses represent over 5 percent of households' total expenditures. Education costs as a percent of household spending are fairly constant across welfare levels. Education expenses are significantly higher in the western provinces, and less in rural areas (refer to figure C.11 in online appendix C).

Physical access to schools

The first requirement for a child to begin education is physical access to schools. Distance to schools is the third most cited reason for children not to attend school. There has been, in fact, no narrowing of the gap in physical access to schools between rural and urban areas or between households of different welfare levels. Access to primary schools is quite high (between 65 and 85 percent for all groups) and increased little between 2011 and 2018. Little difference is seen by wealth quintile. The gap between urban and rural areas remained; increased access occurred only in urban parts of the Western Area (refer to figure C.12 in online appendix C). Access to secondary schools increased from 30 percent to 52 percent between 2011 and 2018, with rates by quintile and urban/rural going up in parallel. In neither year was there a significant difference between urban areas in the Western Area and those elsewhere (refer to figure C.13 in online appendix C).

Poorer students, and those in areas with lower adult schooling/literacy, have less physical access to schools. One can supplement the analysis of physical access to schools from the household survey with more complete information using the 2019 Annual School Census and the 2015 Population and Housing Census to look at the physical distance from each household[12] to a school of each level. Although over 96 percent of households had a primary school within 2 miles as of 2019, those that did not were significantly poorer and disadvantaged in other ways (lower levels of adult literacy and higher rates of farming). Access to a JSS or SSS (within 5 miles) fell to 90 percent and 64 percent, respectively, with similar large differences in the levels of disadvantage between areas with access and those without (refer to figure C.14 in online appendix C).

CONCLUSION

Gains in expected years of education have been very small. There have been slightly larger gains in primary completion rates; however, these gains are concentrated in the middle of distribution, and the poorest, most rural households have not seen a big gain. Access to primary schools has remained flat at fairly high but far from universal levels: only two-thirds of rural households have a primary school within 30 minutes. Bigger gains have been made for secondary schools, but a wide gap remains between rural and urban areas, with only about a third of rural households having a school within 30 minutes. Expense continues to be a big barrier to education. The government's FQSE is a step in the right direction, but it addresses only official school fees and textbooks, which account for only about 20 percent of out-of-pocket education spending for students in public primary and secondary schools. The rollout of the program has benefited schools serving wealthier communities first. More work is needed in the education sector to make sure that poor and rural households benefit.

NOTES

1. Note that this value is higher than the official one (8.9 years) for the World Bank Human Capital Index in 2018. A different methodology is used to calculate expected years of schooling when microdata are available (refer to the text for details).
2. These very high gross enrollment rates (over 100 percent) reflect the presence of many over-age children in primary school, which is not necessarily a good thing.
3. The Western Area is by far the smallest, and it contains the capital city of Freetown and its suburbs outside the city boundaries. Other urban areas within the Western Area consist mainly of a series of towns between the east of Freetown and the city of Waterloo, which form a continuous urban area.
4. The FQSE program started at the beginning of the 2018–19 school year in September 2018. Under the program, the government provides per-student block grants to a subset of public schools so that parents do not have to pay tuition fees. The program started covering about 40 percent of public schools, and increased to about 70 percent by the start of the 2019–20 school year in September 2019.
5. Statistics Sierra Leone, https://www.statistics.sl/index.php/surveys.html.
6. The online appendixes can be found at https://hdl.handle.net/10986/41206.
7. The education sector is managed by the Ministry of Basic and Senior Secondary Education and the Ministry of Technical and Higher Education, with the former responsible for basic (primary and junior secondary school) and senior secondary education and the latter responsible for technical and vocational education and training and higher education.
8. Specifically, Bo, Makeni, Kenema and Koidu.
9. For evidence on how the FQSE has reduced school costs over the first term of the program, refer to chapter 5.
10. Public schools include government, community, and mission schools. They all receive some support from the government and are eligible to be included in the FQSE program.
11. These extra classes may be given by the teachers as a way to supplement their salaries, which are de facto required for students in the classes, or may be classes given by private tutors, which are necessary to make up for the poor quality of instruction at school.
12. Actually, the distance from the center of census enumeration area in which the household lives.

REFERENCES

Barro, R. J. 1991. "Economic Growth in a Cross Section of Countries." *Quarterly Journal of Economics* CVI (425): 407–43.

Kraay, A. 2019. "The World Bank Human Capital Index: A Guide." *World Bank Research Observer* 34 (1): 1–33.

Montenegro, C. E., and H. A. Patrinos. 2014. "Comparable Estimates of Returns to Schooling around the World (English)." Policy Research Working Paper 7020, World Bank, Washington, DC.

Narayan, A., R. Van Der Weide, A. Cojocaru, C. Lakner, S. Redaelli, D. Gerszon Mahler, R. G. N. Ramasubbaiah, and S. H. Thewissen. 2018. *Fair Progress? Economic Mobility across Generations around the World*. Equality and Development Series. Washington, DC: World Bank.

Sen, A. K. 1997. "Editorial: Human Capital and Human Capability." *World Development* 25 (12): 1959–61.

World Bank. 2007. *Education in Sierra Leone: Present Challenges, Future Opportunities*. Washington, DC: World Bank.

World Bank. 2018. *World Development Report 2018: Learning to Realize Education's Promise*. Washington, DC: World Bank.

5 The Immediate Effects of the Free Quality School Education Program

ALEJANDRO DE LA FUENTE, ELIZABETH M. FOSTER, AND HANAN JACOBY

INTRODUCTION

Countries throughout Sub-Saharan Africa have made unprecedented efforts to expand educational enrollment by abolishing/removing direct costs to schooling (school fees), mainly at the primary level (UNESCO 2015). A few countries have recently expanded their free education systems to include secondary school.[1] These policies have been shown to increase educational attainment across a variety of contexts and among the most vulnerable populations (Brudevold-Newman 2017; World Bank 2018b).[2] For instance, the removal of direct costs of schooling through universal primary education in Uganda reduced enrollment fees for most schools, especially in rural areas, and increased primary enrollment by over 60 percent. In Malawi, free primary education increased enrollment by half, favoring girls and poor people (World Bank 2018b).

Sierra Leone is the latest country in the region to aim high for education. Shortly after coming into power in April 2018, the new government announced its flagship policy initiative, the Free Quality School Education Program (FQSE). This program started with the beginning of the 2018–19 school year in September 2018. Under the program, the government provides per-student block grants to public schools that have been approved to receive the transfers (so the grants do not go directly to students), as well as enforcing that such schools do not charge school fees and limiting how much they can charge for other items. The government also provides education materials directly to schools, including textbooks and supplies for students and teachers, and covers exam fees for students sitting the exams administered by West Africa Examination Council. The school feeding program for schools in rural areas is also greatly expanded, with larger amounts provided per student. FQSE aims to support all public schools but started with 39 percent of public schools (representing 59 percent of students) in its first term.

Public messaging by the government on FQSE has stressed decreased costs, increased quality, and increased enrollment as the targeted outcomes of this policy; this analysis considers the immediate effect of such outcomes in the first term of the 2018–19 school year. As the name suggests, FQSE seeks to reduce out-of-pocket spending on education (the "free" component) through eliminating (or at least reducing) school fees and household spending on food through the provision of meals to school-going children. It also seeks to increase the quality of education provided (the "quality" component), particularly through the provision of textbooks for students. Public messaging[3] around the program has also stressed increasing enrollment: parents now have no reason not to send their children to school.

Clearly, there are high expectations from government that the free education program will reduce the financial burden on households and increase coverage (thus, the relevance of exploring some of the preliminary effects of the free education program implemented by the new government). This chapter sets out to understand the effect of the introduction of free schooling on out-of-pocket household expenditures on education and enrollment in the very short term.

The FQSE reform is timely. Challenges in the education sector in Sierra Leone are many: from high out-of-pocket expenditures (refer to chapter 4) to poor learning outcomes and lack of textbooks (and failure to use the ones they have). Most children start their schooling (87 percent of 6-to-17-year-olds have attended school), but very few complete it. Less than half the students who start primary 1 complete primary school, and only about 5 percent complete secondary school (World Bank 2018a). The cost of schooling is the most common reason children drop out of school, and it is also one of the reasons why many children never start school.

The availability of recently collected data on many of the same households *before* the introduction of free education reform and *after* the first school term of implementation (refer to the next section on data and methodology) presents a good opportunity to analyze more thoroughly the immediate effects of free schooling on out-of-pocket expenditures and enrollment. It also allows for tracking the rollout of textbooks and lunches (which are also program components) and the perceptions of the population with regard to the program's performance.

Earlier reports on the impacts of free education in the region largely look at cohorts and focus on the long-term impacts following several years of implementation. This study seeks to fill gaps in our understanding about the effect of free schooling in bringing children back to school and reducing out-of-pocket expenditures over the very short term and the profile of those benefitting at early stages of implementation. Doing so will enable a richer understanding of which school-age populations and households are benefiting from the new program, and it can help in redesigning parts of the program at an early stage to achieve fuller long-term impacts.

The rest of this chapter is organized as follows: The second section describes the data and provides some methodological considerations. The third section introduces the main features of FQSE. The fourth section presents the main effects of free education on welfare and school enrollment. The fifth section concludes by proposing some policy recommendations going forward.

DATA AND METHODOLOGY

The main sources of information for this study are the 2018 Sierra Leone Integrated Household Survey (SLIHS) and the accompanying 2019 Free Quality Education Mobile Phone Survey (FQEMPS). These data were collected by Statistics Sierra Leone, with technical and financial support from the World Bank.[4] The SLIHS is a nationally representative survey; in 2018, it covered 6,840 households, 10 in each of 684 clusters (census enumeration areas [EAs]). The sample is stratified at the district and urban/rural level to allow efficient estimates of poverty rates across these strata.[5] Fieldwork for the SLIHS started in January 2018 and finished in December 2018. The FQEMPS, a follow-up survey to the SLIHS, reinterviewed households covered by the SLIHS via cell phone and in person[6] in February–March 2019; 4,110 of the SLIHS households were reinterviewed.

The SLIHS also collected data on education, including enrollment and expenditures. The enrollment status of every child in the household (including retrospective data on enrollment in each school year going back to the 2013–14 school year) was recorded and, for those currently enrolled, the level (primary school, junior secondary school [JSS], or senior secondary school [SSS]) and the type of school (public or private). The SLIHS also contains the geographic coordinates of all EAs. The recall period for the questions on educational expenses is the past three completed terms, the exact definition of which varied over the 12 months of fieldwork.

The FQEMPS focused on comparing the experiences of students in the first term under FQSE to the first term of the previous school year. The survey began by updating the SLIHS household roster. Questions on education were then asked for all persons in the household ages 5–25. These questions covered enrollment status for 2017–18 and 2018–19, including the level, the exact school attended, and expenses for the first term only of each school year. Additional questions covered the provision of textbooks or school lunches for each student. Finally, the main respondent was asked about their knowledge and perceptions of FQSE.

An innovative feature of the FQEMPS was the possibility to collect the exact school attended by most of the children interviewed. The Annual School Census (ASC) was conducted in July 2018 by the Ministry of Basic and Senior Secondary Education and Statistics Sierra Leone, and contains data on the geographic location of every school in the country along with the level (primary school, JSS, or SSS)[7] and whether the school has the necessary status to receive the per-pupil block grants under FQSE. Data from the ASC were included in the data capture program for the FQEMPS, allowing interviewers to select from a list of nearby schools of the appropriate level for each student, to link the exact school attended by most children with the school census, and to know its status under FQSE.

The authors also combine data from the 2018 and 2019 ASCs, the 2018 SLIHS, and the 2015 Population and Housing Census to create a profile of the catchment area for each school. For each school in the 2019 ASC, the catchment area is defined as a set of census EAs from which the school likely draws its pupils.[8] The authors then compare the catchment areas of public schools that were approved as of the 2019 ASC with those that were not, using data from the 2015 census, as well as estimates of the poverty level of the catchment area, using the methodology developed for the small area estimation of poverty in Sierra Leone (Stats SL and World Bank 2020), using the 2015 census and the 2018 SLIHS.

Although the program was rolled out for only a subset of schools in the first term, there are limitations to comparing beneficiary schools and nonbeneficiary schools using a difference-in-differences framework. As will be shown, the schools that benefited are systematically different from those that did not; the beneficiary schools are older and larger and have better facilities. More important, because of the intensive publicity campaign, many public schools that were not yet benefiting still reduced or eliminated fees, so there is not a pure "control" group. The authors also compare all public schools to private schools (which should not have been affected by the program), but private schools are very different from public schools: they are very concentrated in urban areas and charge fees that are several times higher than those for public schools. A final caveat is that any enrollment changes from one year to the next must be set against the backdrop of an education system that has been rebuilding ever since the end of the civil war. The authors can analyze trends and compare changes between 2016–17 and 2017–18 with changes between 2017–2018 and 2018–19, but the trend cannot be drawn back further, because 2016–17 was the first normal school year after the massive disruptions of the Ebola outbreak.

THE FREE QUALITY SCHOOL EDUCATION PROGRAM

FQSE, which started in September 2018, aims to support schools through a set of benefits to approved public schools in the form of per-pupil block grants to schools, provision of textbooks and school supplies, payment of national examination fees, and a school feeding program.

The benefits are provided directly to the beneficiary schools (in the case of block grants, textbooks, school supplies, and school feeding programs) or exam boards (in the case of exam fees). Benefits accruing to each school depend on the class level and location (urban versus rural). Table 5.1 shows the per-pupil amounts budgeted by the government for these various components over the 2018–19 school year. The block grants provided to the schools are supposed to substitute for the school fees previously collected and cover the miscellaneous running expenses of the school: paying nonteaching personnel (cleaners and others) and teachers who are not on the government payroll, covering minor repairs, and providing basic materials (chalk and ledgers) for teachers.

TABLE 5.1 **Per-student funding under FQSE**

LEVEL	BLOCK GRANTS	TEXTBOOKS	SCHOOL SUPPLIES	EXAM FEES	SCHOOL FEEDING
Preprimary	30,000	18,954	5,926		
Primary	30,000[a]	18,954	5,926	36,000	124,018
Junior secondary	150,000	28,285	8,129	84,000	
Senior secondary	180,000	37,962		108,516	

Source: Ministry of Finance detailed budget for Free Quality School Education (FQSE).

Note: Amounts are shown in Sierra Leonean leones (Le). As of Sept 2019, Le 8,500 = US$1. Exam fees are relevant only for students in the highest class in each level. The school feeding program is for rural areas only.

a. Only Le 15,000 of this amount is new money, because Le 15,000 per pupil in primary school was supposedly previously provided, although there were many gaps in this provision.

The benefits of FQSE are extended to only a subset of public schools (refer to table D.1 in online appendix D)[9] for the first term: approved schools that are set up to receive financial assistance from the government. Schools are "approved" once they have properly registered with the government and meet certain minimum standards, such as submitting photos of buildings, toilets, teachers, and playgrounds. Both public and private schools should complete this process. The process of approving schools has been slow in the recent past, but it is gradually speeding up: as of the 2018 ASC, 11 percent of schools had applied for approval but had not yet been approved. As of June 2019, an additional 324 SSSs, 693 JSSs, and 2,387 preprimary and primary schools had been approved. In order to benefit, the school must also be set up to receive financial support, have submitted its bank details, and have had those details accepted.

According to the 2018 ASC, beneficiary schools to benefit from FQSE in the first term are more established, have better facilities, and are more urban than other public schools (refer to table D.2 in online appendix D). When exploring the correlates of a school becoming approved, the single most important factor from a statistical point of view of whether or not a public school is approved and ready to receive benefits under FQSE is how long it has been in operation. Just 5 percent of public schools less than 10 years old benefited, compared to 27 percent of schools 10–19 years old, and 70 percent of schools 20 or more years old. Forty-nine percent of the public schools in Freetown should benefit, compared to 39 percent in other major towns and 37 percent outside the major towns. The schools slated to benefit from FQSE in the first term also seem to serve a richer body of students, as shown in figure 5.1.

FIGURE 5.1

Physical access to schools, by consumption decile

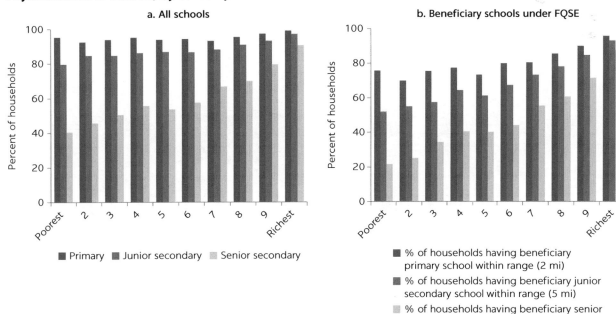

Source: Original calculations using data from the Sierra Leone Annual School Census, 2018, and the Sierra Leone Integrated Household Survey, 2018
Note: The figure shows whether a household has a school of each type within an adequate radius as defined by the World Bank education team: 2 miles for primary school, 5 miles for junior and senior secondary schools. FQSE = Free Quality School Education Program.

As of November 2018, the government of Sierra Leone had disbursed over Le 162 billion of the Le 278 billion budgeted for the first year of FQSE. The money for per-pupil block grants was the first to be disbursed, with most of the money for the first term (Le 28 billion of Le 43 billion) disbursed before schools opened in September. The remaining Le 15 billion were to be disbursed as more schools were classified as "approved" (Massaquoi 2018). Note that the budget for the first year of FQSE (Le 278 billion) is just over half the estimated revenues (of approximately Le 500 billion) anticipated by the government in the form of savings because of recently enacted fuel price liberalization (World Bank and Stats SL 2019). The same recent study estimates that covering all public schools, although not budgeted for in the first year of the program, would cost an additional Le 69 billion.

Poorer households are additionally disadvantaged in terms of physical access to a school benefiting from FQSE. As shown in figure 5.1, poorer households are less likely to have schools of each level nearby (particularly true for SSSs). Once the analysis is broken down into whether or not a school should benefit under FQSE, the discrepancies are even larger and also appear marked at the primary level.

Public knowledge of the program is high, except about the block grants to schools. Most respondents had heard of the program and knew that public schools were not supposed to charge fees. Despite high knowledge of program components, less than 3 percent of respondents mentioned the payment of block grants to schools (refer to table D.3 in online appendix D).

Most households feel they have benefited from the program, with reduced out-of-pocket expenditures on education being the most important benefit across the welfare distribution. Figure 5.2 shows the various benefits reported by households by quintile.[10] Reduced cost is the most important benefit for every quintile. The lower quintiles report benefiting slightly more from being able to send children to school or from worrying less about money than the richer households. Almost a third of households with no school-age or

FIGURE 5.2

Perceived benefits of FQSE, by consumption quintile

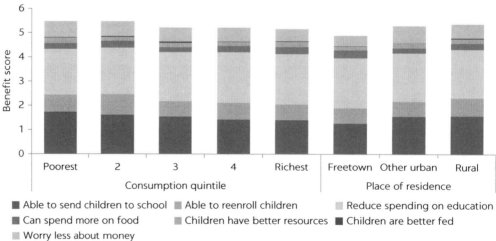

Source: Original calculations using data from the Free Quality Education Mobile Phone Survey, 2019.
Note: The "benefit score" refers to the point total from respondents choosing their three most important benefits, with the most important benefit worth 3 points, the second most important benefit 2 points, and the third most important benefit 1 point. FQSE = Free Quality School Education Program.

school-going children said they benefited from the program—they may have been supporting their children who are not classified as household members (because they live with relatives to attend school) or other extended family members.

RESULTS

Out-of-pocket expenditures

Analysis of changes in school fees will focus on students who attended the same school in 2017–18 as in 2018–19 and on where the breakdown of educational expenses was given. The authors have data on the education of 10,616 children and young adults ages 5–25. Of the 6,378 students enrolled both years, 89 percent continued at the same school (most who changed schools did so because of promotion from one level to the next), giving 5,575 observations with data available on the experiences of the same child at the same school for two different years. The authors have disaggregated information on school expenses (fees versus contributions versus schoolbags versus schoolbooks, and so on) for only a small subset of these students: 1,313 observations.[11] Of these, 97 were not successfully linked to the ASC, so no information is available on the beneficiary status of the school. The resulting final sample consists of 1,216 students. Table D.4 in online appendix D compares this subsample of 1,216 to the full sample of 8,327 children who were in school at least one of the two years. The student sample had a fairly similar coverage to the full sample of students across sociodemographic and school characteristics. In addition, the weights for the analysis in this section were adjusted to correct for this type of nonresponse.

The amount provided by the school fee subsidy block grants is somewhat less than median fees at public primary schools, and slightly more than median fees at public secondary schools. The annual per-pupil subsidy for each level is presented in table D.5 in online appendix D with the distribution of total annual fees (from households interviewed in the main SLIHS, from August 2018 onward, when the recall period for education expenses was the 2017–18 school year) and the distribution of school fees for the first term from the FQEMPS. Schools have different school fee structures; some charge all or most fees when students enroll in the first term, whereas others divide the fees by terms. The government budget for FQSE allocated about 60 percent of the school fees subsidies to be disbursed in the first term.

FQSE has resulted in a decrease in school fees at public schools, both for schools receiving the block grants and for a significant number of those not receiving the grant.[12] The reduction in fees most often took the form of eliminating them, whether the previous fees were above or below the subsidy amount. For primary schools, fees were often above; for JSSs and SSSs, they were usually below.[13] Over 90 percent of public schools of all levels receiving support did not charge fees in 2018–19 (up from about a third of primary schools and almost no JSSs or SSSs in 2017–18).[14] Significant numbers of public schools not receiving support (between 66 and 83 percent) also provided free education, suggesting that they felt pressure (either from the community or the government) not to charge fees, despite the fact that they were not (yet) benefiting. There is little effect on fees charged by private schools, except perhaps a modest decrease in fees for JSSs (refer to table D.6 in online appendix D).[15]

These (fairly large) eliminations and reductions in fees at public schools are statistically significant. Two outcomes are analyzed: whether or not the school is free (does not charge any school fees) and the amount charged as school fees (including free schools as 0). In all cases, a highly significant increase is seen in the likelihood that the school is free, and a decrease in average fees, at both beneficiary and nonbeneficiary public schools. The sample size of private schools is much smaller, and the results are mixed: no significant change in the percent of schools that are free, but a small increase in average fees at primary level (refer to table 5.2).

As table 5.3 shows, the eliminations and reductions in fees are larger at public schools than at private schools, and as large or larger at beneficiary public schools than at nonbeneficiary public schools. The percent of schools eliminating fees is much higher among public schools than at private schools at all levels. Comparing beneficiary public schools to nonbeneficiary public schools, only schools at JSS levels are significantly more likely to reduce fees. The results for average fees are mixed. The reductions are significantly greater at public primary and senior secondary schools compared with private schools but are significantly less at JSSs. The reduction in average fees is significantly greater at beneficiary primary and junior secondary schools compared to nonbeneficiary schools, and less at SSSs.

TABLE 5.2 **Eliminations and reductions of fees**

	PUBLIC NONBENEFICIARY			PUBLIC BENEFICIARY			PRIVATE		
	2017	2018	DIFF	2017	2018	DIFF	2017	2018	DIFF
Percent free									
Primary	21.6	84.1	62.4***	39.8	92.3	52.5***	14.2	19.2	5.0
Junior secondary	4.8	68.3	63.5***	0.5	95.9	95.4***	14.7	29.2	14.5
Senior secondary	0.0	64.2	64.2***	2.8	91.5	88.8***	0.0	12.3	12.3
Average fees									
Primary	37	20	−17***	31	6	−25***	210	224	14***
Junior secondary	105	49	−56***	121	11	−111***	409	255	−154
Senior secondary	174	62	−112***	99	14	−85***	443	637	194

Source: Original calculations using data from the Free Quality Education Mobile Phone Survey, 2019.
Note: Significance level: *** = 1 percent.

TABLE 5.3 **Difference-in-difference of eliminations and reductions of fees across schools**

	DIFFERENCE			DIFFERENCE		
	PUBLIC SCHOOLS	PRIVATE SCHOOLS	DIFF IN DIFF	PUBLIC BENEFICIARY SCHOOLS	PUBLIC NONBENEFICIARY SCHOOLS	DIFF IN DIFF
Increase in percent free						
Primary	55.9	5.0	50.9***	52.5	62.4	−9.9
Junior secondary	83.3	14.5	68.8***	95.4	63.5	31.9***
Senior secondary	81.7	12.3	69.5***	88.8	64.2	24.6
Decrease/increase in average fees						
Primary	−23	14	−37***	−25	−17	−9***
Junior secondary	−90	−154	64***	−111	−56	−55***
Senior secondary	−90	194	−284***	−85	−112	27***

Source: Original calculations using data from the Free Quality Education Mobile Phone Survey, 2019.
Note: Average fee amounts in thousands of Leones. Significance level: *** = 1 percent.

Although almost all beneficiary public schools eliminated fees, nonbeneficiary public schools that had some teachers on the government payroll were significantly more likely to reduce fees. Most beneficiary public schools had at least half their teachers on the government payroll, but only about a quarter of nonbeneficiary public schools did. Not having teachers on the government payroll made it doubly difficult for schools to eliminate fees, because such schools not only did not receive the school fee subsidy but also relied on fees to pay their teachers. Even so, over half of nonbeneficiary schools with no teachers on the payroll eliminated school fees (table D.7 in online appendix D). A logistic-regression analysis looking at the determinants of eliminating fees finds that schools charging lower fees initially were more likely to eliminate them, but it finds no significant difference by level or location.

The elimination of school fees at most public schools provides a significant reduction in out-of-pocket education expenses for households but raises concerns about the sustainability of the program. First, many primary schools will find themselves with significantly lower revenues under FQSE: they are obeying the mandate not to charge fees, but what they get from the government does not make up for the loss of those fees. This problem creates a danger to the sustainability of the program, because schools may resume charging fees or will find other ways to collect money from parents.[16] It may also decrease the quality of education at public primary schools. Second, it is very important to quickly approve all other public schools that are supposed to benefit, because most of these schools have stopped charging school fees and need the government funds to replace those fees. Third, the fee subsidy amounts for secondary schools is more than what many of them were charging, which provides added cash benefit to these schools; it is advisable to monitor how these funds are spent.

Who benefits from reduced out-of-pocket expenditures on education?

The benefits of FQSE through reduced out-of-pocket expenditures on education are spread fairly evenly across the welfare distribution. The authors look at de facto benefits of the program as enacted in the first month. For students attending the same public school in both 2017–18 and 2018–19, the authors assume that school fees would have remained constant in the absence of the program and take the actual difference in fees as the benefit. For students for whom the authors have only the total education expenditure, or who change schools, the median decrease in fees for students at the type (nonbeneficiary public or beneficiary public) and level (primary, JSS, or SSS) of school they attended in 2018–19 is taken as their benefit.

The estimated number of beneficiaries and total value of the reduction in school fees broadly match the government's own estimates of spending and beneficiaries for the program over the first term. Having constructed the actual per-pupil benefit of the program, the authors first compare the total number of beneficiaries and value of benefits to the estimates from the program budget for the first term (table D.8 in online appendix D).[17] Note that the official government budget gives the amount of the subsidy per pupil for different levels, and the total cost of school fee subsidies and number of beneficiaries per level, but the average cost of school fee subsidies per expected beneficiary is much lower than the official per-pupil amount for JSSs and SSSs (Le 67,000 versus Le 150,000 and Le 58,000 versus Le 180,000).

Benefits from FQSE are lowest for the poorest households if gains are measured as share of total benefits. The benefits are relatively evenly distributed by welfare decile, with each decile receiving 8 percent to 12 percent of the benefits; the poorest 20 percent receives the least. This discrepancy is due to lower rates of enrollment (especially at secondary schools, where the cost reductions are greater) and less access to beneficiary schools. Looking at the urban/rural breakdown, households in urban areas outside of Freetown are the biggest beneficiaries as compared to their share of the population. However, as a percentage of total consumption, benefits are highest for the poorest households (refer to table 5.4).

This benefits incidence analysis ignores any enrollment effects of FQSE. Insofar as the program induces children from predominantly poor households to enter or reenter school (some evidence on which is presented in the next section), there may be additional gains concentrated among the bottom deciles. In table 5.4 it is effectively assumed that the marginal child induced to enroll is indifferent between attending or not attending and thus that his or her household's benefit from the program is approximately zero.

Figure 5.3 shows the breakdown of benefits by school level and by beneficiary type for each welfare quintile and place of residence (Freetown, other urban, or rural). The figure shows that each decile benefits fairly equally from reductions/eliminations in fees at primary schools, but the benefits from secondary schools are captured more by richer households. Across the levels and welfare deciles, the benefits households receive come from both beneficiary and nonbeneficiary public schools. Looking by place of residence, rural areas benefit more from fee reductions/eliminations at nonbeneficiary public schools, which are more at risk for being unsustainable.

TABLE 5.4 **Distribution of school fee subsidies, by selected characteristics**

	TOTAL VALUE OF BENEFITS (BILLIONS OF LEONES)	PERCENT OF BENEFITS	TOTAL BENEFITS AS PERCENT OF TOTAL CONSUMPTION (%)
Welfare decile			
Poorest	4.1	7.6	0.54
2	4.6	8.7	0.41
3	5.7	10.7	0.41
4	6.3	11.9	0.38
5	5.8	11.0	0.31
6	5.4	10.2	0.27
7	4.8	9.1	0.21
8	5.5	10.3	0.20
9	5.8	11.0	0.17
Richest	4.7	8.9	0.09
Total	52.8	100	
Geographic location			
Freetown	10.0	18.8	0.14
Other urban	15.8	29.8	0.33
Rural	27.3	51.4	0.25

Source: Original calculations for this publication.
Note: Table shows percent of households as share of total number of households in Freetown (17.9), other urban areas (21.0), and rural areas (61.1).

FIGURE 5.3

Breakdown of benefits, by education level, consumption quintile, and place of residence

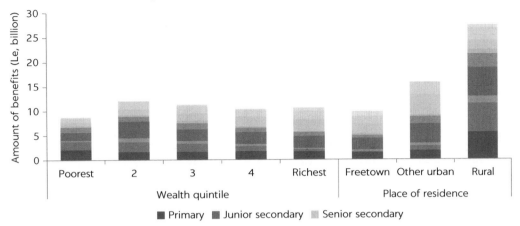

Source: Original calculations for this publication.
Note: For each level, the darkest section represents beneficiary schools, the medium represents nonbeneficiary schools, and the lightest represents public schools of unknown beneficiary status. Le = Sierra Leonean leones.

School enrollment

The effect of FQSE on enrollment in the first term is likely to be limited, and hard to identify empirically. Table D.6 in the online appendix shows that the program lowered fees at *both* beneficiary and nonbeneficiary public schools, and, at the primary level at least, by virtually the same amount. Thus, comparing changes in enrollment or reenrollment rates of primary school-age children at beneficiary schools versus those at nonbeneficiary schools would not be informative about the causal impact of the FQSE. Causal inference is further complicated by preexisting trends in enrollment and the major disruptions due to the Ebola outbreak, which prevent the authors from doing trend analysis. Enrollment rates were already quite high, allowing limited room for dramatic increases in enrollment. The authors look at the possible changes one might see over the first term of FQSE: more young children starting school than in previous cohorts, fewer older children dropping out because of financial pressure, and older children attending school for the first time or reenrolling after an absence of a year or more. In addition, even if overall enrollment does not increase, one might see increased enrollment at public schools compared to private schools or at beneficiary public schools compared to nonbeneficiary public schools.

There is an increase in the proportion of children ages five to seven who started school for the first time. Children in Sierra Leone officially start school at age six, but a significant number of five-year-olds are also enrolled in class 1, and some children do not start until age seven. The authors look at children who were ages five to seven as of August 31, 2018, compared to those ages five to seven as of August 31, 2017, and consider the percent enrolled in primary school. A significant increase is seen in the percent of these young children in school, from 75 percent in 2017 to 81 percent in 2018 (refer to table 5.5). Increases of similar magnitude are found for girls and boys (girls are not disadvantaged at the primary school level; their enrollment rates are as high as, if not higher than, those of boys). The largest enrollment gains are found for the bottom quintile,

TABLE 5.5 **Entrance and reenrollment rates, by education level, gender, consumption quintile, and place of residence**

	5-TO-7-YEAR-OLDS IN CLASS 1			CONTINUATION RATES		
	2017	2018	DIFFERENCE	2017	2018	DIFFERENCE
Overall	74.7	81.3	6.6***	93.1	93.9	0.8
School level						
Primary				95.2	95.7	0.5
Junior secondary				87.3	89.4	2.0
Senior secondary				89.9	89.9	0.0
Gender						
Boys	72.8	81.1	8.3***	93.2	94.4	1.2
Girls	76.6	81.4	4.9**	93.1	93.4	0.4
Consumption quintile						
Poorest	65.7	78.7	13.0***	91.2	93.1	1.9
2	75.6	79.7	4.1	93.0	93.2	0.2
3	73.9	84.9	11.0***	93.4	94.2	0.8
4	81.1	82.1	1.0	95.1	94.7	−0.4
Richest	79.2	81.1	1.8	92.6	94.4	1.8
Geographic location						
Freetown	78.4	80.3	1.9	93.1	95.3	2.2*
Other urban	77.4	84.4	7.0**	93.6	96.1	2.5***
Rural	73.3	80.6	7.3***	92.9	92.7	−0.2
Number of students	1,846	1,793		6,254	6,353	

Source: Original calculations using data from the Free Quality Education Mobile Phone Survey, 2019.
Note: Significance level: * = 10 percent, ** = 5 percent, *** = 1 percent.

with gains for the middle quintile as well. Enrollment shows no significant increase in Freetown; it does so only in other urban areas and rural areas.

A logistic specification, reported in table D.9 in online appendix D, which controls for all the variables in table 5.5 simultaneously, corroborates that enrollment gains are concentrated in the bottom quintile. Importantly, however, these gains may not be attributable directly to FQSE. Enrollment in the five-to seven-year-old cohort increased by 9.5 percentage points between 2016–17 and 2017–18 (analysis of main SLIHS data). Although it is not possible to draw the trend line back any further because 2016–17 was the first normal school year after the disruptions of the Ebola outbreak, the year-on-year enrollment gain uncovered here could simply be part of the post-Ebola recovery. Less obvious is why, if what is occurring is merely the continuation of a broad-based preexisting trend (which it appears to be, because enrollment of five-to seven-year-olds increased across all quintiles the previous year; refer to table D.9 in online appendix D), the enrollment gains in the first year of FQSE were concentrated among the poorest, who are clearly the more sensitive to reductions in school fees.

There is no significant change in the likelihood a child enrolled (up to class SSS2) the previous year will reenroll. No significant change is apparent in continuation rates (table 5.5), except in urban areas, but the limited sample size does not support a multivariate analysis in this case. When households were asked directly why children dropped out between 2017–18 and 2018–19, the most common response was that children failed their exams (23 percent), but the second most common was expense (14 percent). There is little evidence that the reduced costs under FQSE have decreased the percent of students who fail to continue their education.

FQSE may have brought some older students into the school system, as children who had stopped their schooling rejoined. The authors look at children in the 8-to-12-year-old range starting school for the first time (in class 1) or rejoining school and enrolling in class 2 or higher when they were not in school the previous year. There is no difference in the percent of 8-to-12-year-olds starting school (which was already quite high: over a quarter of out-of-school 8-to-12-year-olds enroll). The rate of 8-to-12-year-olds rejoining school increased from almost none to 4 percent,[18] with the largest increases seen for boys, those in the poorest quintile, and Freetown (refer to table D.10 in online appendix D). Note that, although these results are statistically significant, they are based on very small sample sizes. In terms of raw counts, one can see that 4 students ages 8–12 rejoined in 2017 and 14 in 2018.

The analysis finds little evidence that children moved from one school to another to take advantage of FQSE or for any other reason. Only 3 percent of primary school students, 5 percent of JSS students, and 6 percent of SSS students changed schools. (These shares represent only 213 students in the sample, so the following analysis is based on a very small sample.) Overall, the most common reason given for changing schools was that the new school was perceived as being of better quality; next most common was that the child moved. There is no obvious pattern of students moving from schools that did not benefit under FQSE to those that did; just as many students moved from those that did benefit to those that did not.

The percent of children attending public (as opposed to private) schools increased modestly, although the rate was very high to begin with, but no evidence exists of movement from nonbeneficiary public schools to beneficiary schools. Even if children do not switch schools, one still might see the fraction of children at public schools (or beneficiary public schools) increase, because new students are more likely to start at those schools, or students are more likely to reenroll if they had been at those schools. The fraction of children attending public schools increases slightly from 93.9 percent to 94.1 percent, with significant changes at the primary level and in the second decile. The percent of public school students at beneficiary public schools did not change significantly and appears to decrease for SSS students (refer to table D.11 in online appendix D).

Net and gross enrollment rates changed little between 2017–18 and 2018–19. Net enrollment increased for primary school and decreased for JSS and SSS, but only the decrease for SSS is statistically significant. The authors also break the analysis down by sex, wealth quintile, and urban/rural, finding no particular pattern to the results. Looking over these 10 different subgroups, the analysis finds four significant increases for primary net enrollment and one significant decrease for SSS net enrollment. Gross enrollment rates follow roughly the same pattern—most of the changes are not significant. Again, a decrease for boys in SSS is seen (refer to tables D.12 and D.13 in online appendix D).

There are a number of reasons why only modest increases are seen in enrollment in the first year. First, enrollment levels were already quite high, with 87 percent of children starting school. Of those who did not start school, the most common reason was lack of interest/usefulness. If FQSE manages to improve the quality of education and learning outcomes, it may change this attitude, but only slowly over time. The second reason given is expense. Although FQSE has significantly decreased out-of-pocket expenditures, the cost of education in school fees, school uniforms, and supplies may still be a significant barrier for some households (for a discussion of different types of user fees in primary education across multiple settings, refer to Bentaouet-Kattan and Burnett 2004). In addition, parents may not believe that the program will really ensure lower-cost education in the long run; they may make their own financial contribution (purchasing uniforms or supplies) only to find that the school demands payment in other forms or that fees reappear later in the school year or in the subsequent year. Some households still lack physical access to a primary school; universal primary education will not be achieved until that problem is remedied.

Equity impact of FQSE

To further understand whether FQSE is reaching students in the most underserved areas, data are also combined from the 2018 and 2019 ASCs, the 2018 SLIHS, and the 2015 census to create a profile of the catchment area for each school. For each school in the 2019 ASC, a catchment area is defined as a set of census EAs from which the school likely draws its pupils.[19] It is possible then to compare the catchment areas of public schools that were approved as of the 2019 ASC and those that were not, using data from the 2015 census, as well as estimates of the poverty level of the catchment area, using the methodology developed for the small area estimation of poverty in Sierra Leone (Stats Sierra Leone and World Bank 2019, 2020), using the 2015 census and the 2018 SLIHS.

Schools that receive funding under FQSE serve less poor, more advantaged catchment areas than those that have not yet been approved to receive funding. Overall, the catchment areas of approved public schools had higher rates of adult literacy, child school attendance, and adults who had ever attended school than those of unapproved public schools. They have lower rates of households engaged in agriculture and of those in poverty and extreme poverty. These gaps are largest for primary schools but are also very apparent for SSSs. They tend to be smaller or almost nonexistent for JSSs (refer to figure D.1 in online appendix D).

Over half of the nonapproved schools in 2018 had been approved by 2019, but even this process favors schools serving those who are better off. The Ministry of Basic and Senior Secondary Education moved quickly over the 2018–19 school year to approve more public schools and get them set up to receive funding under this program. Considering public schools that were not approved as of September 2018, over half had been approved by the 2019–20 school year. However, when the authors compare schools that managed to gain approval over this year with those that did not, primary schools and SSSs that gained approval served a more advantaged pool of students—that is, students from areas with higher adult literacy, higher child and adult school attendance, lower rates of occupation in agriculture, and lower rates of poverty. For JSSs, there is little difference on most of these measures, and the schools that did manage to gain approval actually serve more agricultural and poor communities (refer to figure D.2 in online appendix D).

Who benefits from textbooks and school lunches?

School lunches under FQSE have not been rolled out in a significant way. The school feeding program was supposed to target primary schools in rural areas.

Only about 17 percent of children at these schools reported receiving lunch. As many or more students at nonbeneficiary public schools or in urban areas (outside of Freetown) reported receiving lunch (refer to table D.14 in online appendix D). The 2018 ASC collected information on whether or not the school had a school feeding program (before the advent of FQSE). There is no correlation between whether the school reported having a school feeding program and whether the households reported that children received lunch at school. Students from the poorest backgrounds did benefit more from school meals than did other groups. Almost two-thirds of the students receiving lunch get it five days a week, another 17 percent get it three days a week. The food is not perceived to be of particularly high quality; over half the parents say it is worse than what their kids would eat at home.

Over 50 percent of students at beneficiary public secondary schools report having textbooks they can take home to use. For primary schools, this share is 10 percent (refer to table D.15 in online appendix D). The authors did not ask where students had textbooks during 2016–17, but the survey did ask specifically about whether students were given their own textbooks to take home and use— the major innovation of the FQSE.[20] Although the distribution of textbooks is not supposed to differ by urban/rural, somewhat higher rates of receiving books are seen outside of Freetown. Over two-thirds of the students with textbooks have exactly two books: a math book and an English book.

CONCLUSION

The reduction in fees for primary and secondary education through block grants to approved schools, together with a massive program of dissemination and awareness, has been effective in reducing out-of-pocket expenditures. Some evidence also suggests increasing primary attendance for the first time by the poorest children, but this increase cannot unambiguously be attributed to the program because of preexisting trends in school entry and the fact that both beneficiary and nonbeneficiary schools lowered or eliminated fees. These findings nevertheless give rise to the hope that these gains can be consolidated and expanded into the rest of the population. Other gains are yet to be seen beyond the immediate scope of the program, such as rolling out textbooks and free meals extensively, increasing retention rates, and eliminating the gender bias at the secondary level. Furthermore, the positive effects on out-of-pocket household expenditures could add problems ahead in ensuring that decreases of funding to schools do not erode the gains from the program.

There are a number of implications of the fact that schools not benefiting from the program have reduced or eliminated fees and that, for many primary schools, the reduction in fees enacted is larger than the per-pupil block grants received. First, as noted earlier, many primary schools will find themselves with significantly lower revenues under FQSE: the grant amounts do not cover the lost income for schools that obey the mandate not to charge fees. Lower revenues may lead schools to resume charging fees or collecting money in other ways, threatening the sustainability of the program, and may also decrease the quality of education. Second, because most schools have stopped charging school fees, it is important to quickly approve other public schools and get funds to them. The funds allocated for the first year (Le 278 B) of the FQSE are only half the estimated savings from the fuel price liberalization (Le 500 billion over the first year), so the program can be scaled up.

FQSE should be scaled up and focus on rapidly approving public schools serving poor and remote communities and also consider increasing the level of support provided to primary schools. Owing to their higher rates of enrollment in secondary school and better access to approved public schools, richer households benefit more than poor ones from the per-student block grants. Moreover, the fee subsidy amount for secondary schools is more than most of them were charging, thus providing a cash benefit to the schools, which could be used to enhance quality. Nevertheless, it may be advisable to monitor how these funds are spent.

Future monitoring of the program at the household level will be necessary in order to see that fee reductions are maintained once the initial burst of publicity is over and to see whether longer-term expected results, such as increased retention and better learning outcomes, materialize.

NOTES

1. Secondary school fees were eliminated in Uganda (2007), Rwanda (2007, 2012), and Tanzania (2016); for girls in The Gambia (2001–04); and selectively for schools in relatively poorer areas in South Africa (2007).

2. Refer to, for example, the analysis of programs in Kenya (Lucas and Mbiti 2012), Malawi (Al-Samarrai and Zaman 2007), Tanzania (Hoogeveen and Rossi 2013), and Uganda (Deininger 2003; Grogan 2009; Nishimura, Yamano, and Sasaoka 2008).

3. For example, KME All Stars created the official music video "Education Na Free," available at https://www.youtube.com/watch?v=wKGDw7y5CZQ; and the Ministry of Basic and Secondary Education released a music video, "Free Education Song," available at https://www.youtube.com/watch?v=c8NV2Xx93iA. These songs and others have received extensive play time on radio throughout Sierra Leone.

4. This is the third round of this survey; previous rounds were conducted in 2003–04 and 2011.

5. SLIHS is also the source of detailed information on household consumption and expenditure for calculation of the main welfare indicator. The main indicator of welfare is per adult equivalent household consumption as calculated from the SLIHS 2018. It includes five main components: food consumption (comprising purchases, consumption of own production, and gifts/free food), nonfood expenditure (covering a wide range of items, including fuel and transportation), expenditure on health and education, housing, and use value of durable goods. Detailed information on the construction of consumption aggregate and the poverty line can be found in Stats SL and World Bank (2019).

6. Households in Freetown and in 58 remote EAs with low cell phone coverage were interviewed in person. The authors attempted to call all other households that had provided a cell phone on the main SLIHS. Response rates for in-person interviews were high (1,307 of 1,440 in Freetown and 579 of 580 in remote areas) but only about 70 percent for cell phone calls owing to failure to get through on many of the numbers provided. The weights in the data have been adjusted to correct for this nonresponse.

7. Primary schools are usually separate institutions from secondary schools, and junior and secondary schools are also often separate. When one institution covers two or more levels, it appears as multiple observations in the census.

8. This definition includes all EAs whose center point is within a given radius—2 miles for primary schools and 5 miles for secondary schools—and all EAs for which that school is the closest one (or one of the roughly equally close ones) of that level (primary school, JSS, or SSS). As a robustness check, the authors also did the analysis using the chiefdom section in which the school is located as the catchment area; the results are very similar. These catchment areas can overlap, and they do so extensively in urban areas.

9. The online appendixes can be found at https://hdl.handle.net/10986/41206.

10. Households provided up to three benefits in order of importance; the most important benefit is assigned 3 points, and so on.

11. As on the main SLIHS, the interviewer had the option to either enter the breakdown of school expenses in 10 categories—school fees, mandatory contributions, uniforms, schoolbooks, schoolbag, stationery, transportation, food and lodging at boarding school, extra classes, and other—or just have respondents estimate the total if they could not provide the breakdown. Implementing the question in Survey Solutions, it was necessary to add a filter question first as to whether or not the respondent could provide the breakdown. Doing so resulted in only the total being given much more often on the FQEMPS, especially for the 2017–18 school year, than on the main SLIHS.

12. Note that the assignment of schools as beneficiaries or nonbeneficiaries may not be perfect. First, it is based on the whether the school *should* receive benefits according to the 2018 ASC. This determination was not checked against any list of actual disbursements to schools. Second, there may be some cases in which the school attended by the child was not correctly identified by the interviewer. Both of these sources of error should be fairly small.

13. Note that the comparison is of annual subsidies with changes in fees for the first term.

14. The authors also asked households directly if anyone from the school or the school management committee asked for any mandatory contribution for school fees or textbooks. Even for schools that charged fees, only just over a third of respondents reported being asked directly. A significant number of households with children in public schools who did not pay fees or mandatory contributions reported being asked for them (16 percent of non-beneficiary public schools and 9 percent of beneficiary public schools), suggesting either that parents were empowered to push back and refuse to pay fees at public schools even when asked, or that they paid something that was not captured in the question on school expenses.

15. Three private JSSs, all run by Muslim organizations, eliminated fees for 2018–19; these schools drive the results for JSSs.

16. There is no evidence of price discrimination—that is, schools charging wealthier households more. Because of the clustered nature of the original data, there are multiple observations for many schools in the data set, either from children within the same household or from households within the same census EA (or even another census EA in urban areas). For the first term of 2018–19, the authors have information on school fees for 1,244 schools. Of these, there are observations from multiple households for 429 of them, with an average of four children from three different households attending each school. Analysis of the fees paid by these students shows no evidence of price discrimination. Children from wealthier and poorer households attending the same schools report paying roughly the same fees, which implies that the benefits of the program are equally distributed within schools.

17. Note that the government allocated about 60 percent of the total fee subsidies for the first term, perhaps reflecting the practice that a larger fraction of school fees is collected by schools in the first term.

18. This rate varies little with age, staying at about this level until age 12.

19. Refer to endnote 8 for a discussion of the methodology used regarding catchment areas.

20. Previously, textbooks tended to be shared among students and kept at the school.

REFERENCES

Al-Samarrai, S., and H. Zaman. 2007. "Abolishing School Fees in Malawi: The Impact on Education Access and Equity." *Education Economics* 15 (3): 359–75.

Bentaouet-Kattan, R., and N. Burnett. 2004. "User Fees in Primary Education." Education for All Working Paper, World Bank, Washington, DC.

Brudevold-Newman, A. 2017. *The Impacts of Free Secondary Education: Evidence from Kenya.* College Park: University of Maryland.

Deininger, K. 2003. "Does Cost of Schooling Affect Enrollment by the Poor? Universal Primary Education in Uganda." *Economics of Education Review* 22 (3): 291–305.

Grogan, L. 2009. "Universal Primary Education and School Entry in Uganda." *Journal of African Economies* 18 (2): 183–211.

Hoogeveen, J., and M. Rossi. 2013. "Enrolment and Grade Attainment Following the Introduction of Free Primary Education in Tanzania." *Journal of African Economies* 22 (3): 375–93.

Lucas, A. M., and I. M. Mbiti. 2012. "Access, Sorting, and Achievement: The Short Run Effects of Free Primary Education in Kenya." *American Economic Journal: Applied Economics* 4 (4): 226–53.

Massaquoi, M. E. 2018. "Sierra Leone Government Allocates Le 43 Billion for School Fees." *Sierra Leone Telegraph*, September 7, 2018. https://www.thesierraleonetelegraph.com /sierra-leone-government-allocates-le43-billion-for-school-fees/.

Nishimura, M., T. Yamano, and Y. Sasaoka. 2008. "Impacts of the Universal Primary Education Policy on Educational Attainment and Private Costs in Rural Uganda." *International Journal of Educational Development* 28 (2): 161–75.

Stats SL (Statistics Sierra Leone). 2019. *2018 Sierra Leone Integrated Household Survey (SLIHS) Report*. Freetown: Statistics Sierra Leone.

Stats SL (Statistics Sierra Leone) and World Bank. 2019. "Methodology for Consumption-Poverty Estimation, 2018 and Poverty Trends, 2011–2018, in Sierra Leone." Stats SL and World Bank, Freetown, Sierra Leone. https://www.statistics.sl/images/StatisticsSL /Documents/SLIHS2018/SLIHS_2018_New/SLIHS_2018_Methodology_Note_for _Poverty_Calculations.pdf.

Stats SL (Statistics Sierra Leone) and World Bank. 2020. "Subnational Poverty Estimates for Sierra Leone." World Bank, Washington, DC.

UNESCO (United Nations Educational, Scientific, and Cultural Organization). 2015. *Education for All 2000–2015: Achievements and Challenges*. Education for All Global Monitoring Report.

World Bank. 2018a. "Free Quality Education. Analysis and Future Support Directions." PowerPoint Presentation by Education GP for the Human Capital Project.

World Bank. 2018b. *World Development Report 2018: Learning to Realize Education's Promise*. Washington, DC: World Bank.

World Bank and Statistics Sierra Leone. 2019. *Impact of Fuel Price Liberalization on Poverty and Inequality in Sierra Leone*. Washington, DC: World Bank.

6 The Power of Investing in Girls
ENDING CHILD MARRIAGE AND PROMOTING GIRLS' EDUCATION

QUENTIN WODON, CHATA MALE, ADENIKE ONAGORUWA, MARI SHOJO, AND ANTONINO GIUFFRIDA

INTRODUCTION

In many low-income countries, despite substantial progress over the past two decades, girls have, on average, less secondary education than boys (on West Africa, refer to Male and Wodon 2018). In Sierra Leone, girls do as well as boys in terms of gross enrollment and completion rates at the primary education level, but they lag behind substantially in secondary education. Moreover, on average, boys perform better in secondary education learning assessments than girls.[1] In the case of educational attainment, one of the factors leading to gender gaps is that, before they are 18, a significant proportion (up to a third) of girls marry or have children, thus compromising their opportunities to enroll in or complete secondary school (on girls' own voices on those issues in Sierra Leone, refer to Street Child 2016). Although other factors related to the supply of and demand for education may also affect gender gaps in educational attainment, child marriage and early childbearing play a major role. They also have a range of other negative impacts, because girls are marrying or having children before they are physically and emotionally ready. Giving girls more educational opportunities and reducing rates of child marriage and early childbearing are essential to ensure that girls have full agency not only as future wives and mothers but also in a vast range of other roles, including in the job market. Making such changes is essential for Sierra Leone to reach its full development potential.

Disadvantages faced by girls were likely exacerbated by the recent COVID-19 crisis (on the pandemic and policy responses for the education sector, refer to World Bank 2020b). The crisis led to massive school closures globally, affecting 1.6 billion students according to the United Nations Educational, Scientific and Cultural Organization. School closures may cause not only loss of learning for most students in the short term but also diminished economic opportunities and losses in human capital over the long term. Risks of not returning to school are especially high for adolescent girls, who may become married or pregnant while out of school. The health crisis also led to an economic crisis, with

Sub-Saharan Africa experiencing its first recession in 25 years. Sierra Leone is also being affected. What may be the magnitude of the consequences of the crisis for children? Although the COVID-19 crisis differed from the Ebola epidemic that affected Sierra Leone in 2014, the experience of the Ebola outbreak suggests that impacts on the education system and learners may be severe (United Nations 2020). Research on the effect of the Ebola pandemic shows that thousands of girls were left vulnerable and that there were increases in unwanted and transactional sex for food. Girls were more likely to drop out of school than boys in the areas most affected by the Ebola epidemic.

Beyond the potential impact of the COVID-19 crisis, despite great progress since the end of the civil war, Sierra Leone continues to be confronted by massive challenges related to child marriage, early childbearing, and low educational attainment for girls. Although girls perform as well as boys at the primary level, they lag behind at the secondary level. Primary completion rates for girls are relatively high in Sierra Leone, increasing massively over the past few decades, thanks in part to the end of the civil war. Gains for secondary education were also large, especially at the lower-secondary level. However, although almost three in four girls complete their primary education, only one in two completes lower-secondary education, and fewer than one in five completes upper secondary.

There has been only limited progress in reducing child marriage and early childbearing. The prevalence of child marriage among girls ages 18–22 was 28.2 percent in the 2017 Multi-Indicator Cluster Survey (analysis in this chapter also relies on the 2013 Demographic and Health Survey; a more detailed and updated analysis using the 2019 Demographic and Health Survey is to come in Wodon, forthcoming). Higher levels are observed for older women, but gains over time have been limited. For early childbearing, the prevalence among girls ages 18–22 was 29.1 percent, slightly higher than for child marriage, suggesting that quite a few cases of early childbearing take place outside of marriage. Reductions over time in the prevalence of early childbearing have also been small.

The analysis provided in the rest of this chapter makes the case for better and more investments in adolescent girls, especially to improve education outcomes and reduce child marriage and early childbearing. In terms of structure, the rest of this chapter is organized as follows: The second section discusses the relationships between child marriage, early childbearing, and low educational attainment for girls. The third section documents the negative impacts on other development outcomes of low educational attainment for girls and either child marriage or early childbearing (depending on the indicator). The fourth section estimates a few of the economic costs associated with those impacts (cost-of-inaction analysis). The fifth section considers some of the policy interventions that could help end child marriage and early childbearing and promote better educational opportunities for girls. The sixth section concludes.

METHODOLOGY AND FRAMEWORK

The framework that guides the analysis (Wodon et al. 2018) recognizes that there is a close relationship between girls' educational attainment, child marriage, and, as a result, early childbearing. Ensuring that girls remain in school is one of the best ways to delay marriage and thereby reduce childbearing, with beneficial effects on Sierra Leone's development indicators. By contrast, marrying early or becoming pregnant leads girls to drop out of school. Furthermore, child marriage is one of the main drivers of early childbearing.

In turn, both girls' educational attainment and child marriage and early childbearing matter for other development outcomes. Four main outcomes are considered: (1) fertility; (2) health, including nutrition and the risk of exposure to intimate partner violence; (3) work, including labor force participation and earnings; and (4) agency, including decision-making and other impacts. Although some impacts are estimated for the girls marrying or dropping out of school early, others are estimated for their children. Note that in some cases the authors look at the impact of child marriage and in other cases at the impact of early childbearing, depending on what the relationships are, based on the literature.

The analysis then estimates selected economic costs of inaction or, equivalently, the benefits associated with ending child marriage and early childbearing or educating girls. The language of costs and benefits is used interchangeably. Examples of benefits from offering girls better educational opportunities, ending child marriage, and preventing early childbearing include (1) increased growth in gross domestic product (GDP) per capita as a result of reduced population growth, (2) higher labor earnings for women in adulthood, (3) increased labor earnings for children in adulthood due to reductions in stunting, (4) valuation of the benefits associated with children's lives saved, and (5) reduced budget needs as the rate of population growth falls. Though far from exhaustive, this list identifies those examples with the largest expected economic benefits.

Finally, the analysis recognizes that the benefits derived from providing girls with improved educational opportunities and eliminating child marriage at the individual and household levels have broader implications nationally and even globally. By raising standards of living (through higher GDP per capita, lower population growth, and higher earnings for women), educating girls and ending child marriage will reduce both poverty and inequality.

The objective of this chapter is to estimate the impacts of child marriage, early childbearing, and educational attainment for girls on a wide range of development outcomes and the economic costs associated with some of these impacts. The term *impact* is used for the sake of simplicity, but caution is called for in inferring causality. The interactions between multiple outcomes considered in this chapter are such that there is a risk of reverse causality in some of the empirical estimations. Although efforts have been undertaken to reduce such risks, estimates of impacts in this chapter are typically obtained through regression analysis to estimate the potential impacts of child marriage, early childbearing, or educational attainment on various outcomes, while controlling for other factors that may also affect the outcomes. In the literature, this approach is known as an "association study." Only statistical associations are measured, not necessarily the impacts that could be observed with a randomized controlled trial or quasi-experimental approaches. Based on measures of likely impacts, the costs associated with some of them (cost-of-inaction approach or, equivalently, the benefits of ending child marriage/early childbearing and educating girls) are computed. The estimates are based on debatable assumptions, including in some cases, discount rates. It should therefore be recognized that the cost estimates are not precise—they simply represent an order of magnitude of potential costs.

In addition, the estimates of the costs of child marriage in terms of unrealized potential earnings implicitly assume that labor markets would be able to absorb a larger supply of better-educated women. Specifically, the assumption is that the higher educational attainment resulting from eliminating child marriage would not decrease the returns to education. However, if eliminating child marriage were to substantially increase the average level of women's education, that assumption might be questionable, especially in a country where a very large proportion of women currently have minimal education. The estimation also does not factor in possible effects on men's earnings if, on average, women acquire more education; if more women achieve higher levels of education and have access to the same employment opportunities as men, that would reduce the occupational segregation by sex that has traditionally led to relatively higher earnings for men.

There is evidence from other economies that over time the labor market premiums associated with more education may decline when the proportion of workers with these higher levels increases. For example, Angrist (1995) showed that expansion of access to education in West Bank and Gaza reduced the skills premium. Acemoglu, Autor, and Lyle (2004) noted that, during World War II, higher labor force participation by women depressed wages for low-skilled workers. Duflo (2004) suggested similar effects in Indonesia after a large school construction program. These are just a few examples of studies that document general equilibrium effects, which, as noted by Acemoglu (2010), can be large. In a World Bank study on the cost of not educating girls globally (Wodon et al. 2018), those potential general equilibrium effects were accounted for by providing a variety of estimates, with and without general equilibrium effects. This consideration seems less necessary when looking at the impacts of child marriage in Sierra Leone, because only a subset of women marrying early are assumed to complete secondary education without marrying as a child, given other constraints, such as cost or the distance to schools. Changes in earnings due to elimination of child marriage generally average about 1 percent of aggregate wages. Thus, the impact on the labor market remains limited, so we are less likely to observe large general equilibrium effects.

Still, if general equilibrium effects occur, the estimates provided may be overstating the cost of child marriage in terms of lost earnings. However, other factors could lead to larger costs than reported: First, the estimation does not factor in possible effects of ending child marriage on labor force participation or hours worked. Second, through multiplier effects, increasing women's earnings through better educational opportunities could generate larger gains for both men and women than are suggested here. Finally, intergenerational benefits from higher earnings for women, such as better education for their children or other benefits associated with better education for women, are also not factored in. In the long run, gains from ending child marriage could thus be larger than suggested by earnings regressions that capture current conditions.

Relationships between child marriage, early childbearing, and girls' education

The relationships between child marriage, early childbearing as one of its consequences, and girls' education are complex, with a multitude of drivers. A cursory look at the data across countries in West Africa makes the relationships clear. Consider, for example, the relationship between child marriage and girls' education. As discussed in Wodon, Male, and Onagoruwa. (2020), lower-secondary level completion rates are associated with a higher prevalence rate for child marriage, with variations in child marriage accounting for almost 60 percent of the variation between countries in lower-secondary school completion. Keeping girls in secondary school is an important factor in ending child marriage—a conclusion overwhelmingly supported by the literature.

The close relationship between the prevalence of child marriage and girls' educational attainment can also be illustrated by a simple typology of adolescent girls according to their marriage and schooling status. The results suggest that after a certain age, girls are either married or in school, but not both, because only 1.6 percent of the sample consists of girls who are married and in school. Owing to social norms and parental pressure related in part to the out-of-pocket and opportunity costs of schooling, many girls may feel pressure to marry, in which case they essentially can't remain in school. Child marriage thus reduces girls' educational prospects; conversely, more education (and employment) opportunities for girls reduce the likelihood that they will marry early. A full discussion of the related issues is beyond the scope of this chapter; however, later the authors draw on the literature to recommend some policy options to delay marriage and childbearing.

In addition, child marriage is closely correlated with (and likely to be the cause of) almost two-thirds of all cases of early childbearing (a girl having her first child before the age of 18) and childbirth (a child born to a mother younger than 18). Estimations suggest that close to two-thirds of instances of early childbearing can be attributed to child marriage. The analysis is based on the timing of marriages and births. In about a third of cases, early childbearing may precede child marriage, but this timing is less likely in Sierra Leone than the reverse. Still, in comparison to various other countries in East Africa and South Asia, the share of instances of early childbearing due to child marriage in Sierra Leone and the other West African countries is often lower, suggesting that other actions beyond preventing child marriages are needed to prevent early pregnancies.

Keeping girls in school significantly reduces the risks of child marriage and early childbearing. When surveys ask why their daughters dropped out of school, or when education management information systems collect and include such information, parents often attribute their daughters dropping out of school to marriage and pregnancies. Experimental data, as well as regression analysis across countries, also suggest that child marriage affects educational attainment negatively (refer to, for example, Field and Ambrus 2008; Nguyen and Wodon 2014; Wodon, Nguyen, and Tsimpo 2016). The causality may run both ways, in that lack of educational attainment may lead to child marriage as well as early childbearing. In the case of Sierra Leone, estimates based on data from the 2013 Demographic and Health Survey and controlling for a range of other factors, including household wealth, suggest that each additional year of secondary education may reduce the risk of child marriage by 10.0 percentage points. This estimate is larger than what is observed in many other countries.

In addition, each additional year of secondary education may reduce the risk of early childbearing by 4.0 percentage points, which is in line with estimates for other countries. Conversely, for each year of delay in marriage before the age of 18, there is an increase in secondary school enrollment of 2.6 percentage points, although the effect on the completion of secondary school is not statistically significant. Finally, across generations, by reducing the educational attainment of girls, child marriage and early childbearing reduce the opportunities available to their children. Children born to young mothers with low levels of education or no education at all are themselves significantly more likely to acquire less education. The importance of keeping girls in school to end child marriage is discussed in the following sections when reviewing interventions that may help delay marriage.

Given the close correlation between educational attainment, child marriage, and early childbearing, one of the most effective interventions to reduce the prevalence of child marriage and early childbearing would seem to be incentives for girls to remain in or go back to school. In particular, universal secondary completion for girls could dramatically reduce the prevalence of child marriage and early childbearing. Eliminating child marriage and early childbearing would help to improve girls' average educational attainment; however, that alone would not be sufficient to ensure achievement of universal secondary education completion. A later section discusses policy options for keeping girls in school, but the end of the ban for pregnant girls to stay in school is a positive step.

IMPACTS ON DEVELOPMENT OUTCOMES

Fertility and population growth

Child marriage, early childbearing, and girls' education have a significant impact on how many children women bear, and thus on population growth. According to a model adopted from Onagoruwa and Wodon (2018), the earlier women in Sierra Leone and elsewhere marry, the more likely they are to bear children earlier and ultimately to have a larger number of children. Depending on the age at marriage, child marriage increases the average number of children women bear (total fertility) by 9 to 28 percent in Sierra Leone. Consequently, eliminating child marriage could reduce the national fertility rate by 8 percent (a reduction in fertility of 0.45 child per woman nationally). Universal completion of secondary education would in addition reduce total fertility rates by 12.7 percent. Although ending child marriage would not increase the use of modern contraceptives in Sierra Leone, the potential impact of universal secondary education completion would be large (increase of 41.1 percent as compared with the baseline value, which corresponds to an increase of 6.7 percentage points).

Estimates provided in the World Bank (2020a) economic report for Sierra Leone on which this chapter is based suggest that the elimination of child marriage and early childbearing in Sierra Leone could reduce the annual rate of population growth by 0.14 percentage point—a reduction in the annual rate of population growth of about 7 percent from the base value (population growth rate of 2.1 percent).[2] This estimate is similar in magnitude to the estimated reduction in total fertility (refer to the methodology section on what is meant by *impacts*). Even greater reductions could be achieved if all girls completed secondary education, with the effects likely to be at least one and a half times larger. These effects have implications for Sierra Leone's ability to reap the benefits from the demographic dividend (for a detailed discussion of the dividend, refer to Canning, Raja, and Yazbeck 2015; World Bank 2015). The reduction in population growth and fertility rates also has implications for the reduction of the youth dependency ratio and the demographic dividend, thus leading to increased productivity and poverty reduction because poverty is estimated on the basis of household consumption per capita or per equivalent adult. Because household sizes shrink when fertility rates drop, the risk of being poor or falling into poverty is accordingly reduced. As mentioned in World Bank (2020a), the incidence of poverty is projected to increase in Sierra Leone because of the COVID-19 crisis, with the number of poor increasing even further with population growth. If population growth and fertility rates were to fall by reducing child marriage and early childbearing, poverty could be reduced more rapidly.

Health, nutrition, and violence

Early childbearing can significantly undermine the health and nutrition of both young mothers and their children. For the young mothers, physical immaturity may increase the likelihood of complications during pregnancy and childbirth, exacerbating maternal mortality and morbidity risks, although those risks are not measured here (for estimates of maternal mortality, refer to, for example, Nove et al. 2014). In Sierra Leone, maternal-related deaths accounted for 19.8 percent of deaths among women ages 15–19, and complications during pregnancy and childbirth are the second most common cause of death for 15-to-19-year-old girls.

Being born to a very young mother may also affect the health and nutrition of the child at a time that is critical for the child's development; the evidence is overwhelming that children's health during their first 1,000 days has a lifelong impact. These impacts are reviewed by Black et al. (2017) and for child marriage by Wodon (2016). For example, stunting in early childhood is associated with lower lifelong earnings and consumption for both individuals and their households (Hoddinott et al. 2013) and with losses in national GDP (Horton and Steckel 2013). In Sierra Leone, children born of mothers younger than 18 have substantially higher risks of dying before they reach the age of five,[3] but the impact on stunting is not statistically significant. However, the reductions in under-five mortality that could result from preventing early childbearing nationally are limited in percentage terms because relatively few children are born of mothers younger than 18 (even for girls having their first child before the age of 18, most of the children they will have over their lifetime will be after they reach the age of 18). Still, many children would be affected. The impact of educational attainment for girls on both under-five mortality and stunting is not statistically significant for most levels of education, including completion of secondary education. Separately, although the impact of child marriage on intimate partner violence was not estimated for Sierra Leone, based on data for other countries in the region, the impact is expected to be statistically significant though relatively small (Savadogo and Wodon 2018; also refer to Onyango et al. 2019.). The impact for educational attainment may be larger.

Work, earnings, and poverty

The elimination of child marriage could have impacts on labor force participation because child marriage affects girls' education and total fertility, although the impacts are likely to be small. However, the impact of the elimination of child marriage on the earnings of adult women could be more significant.

Women who married early could have earned more if they had married later, mostly because of the impact of child marriage on their education. Nationally, this change could raise the population's total earnings by 0.7 percentage point.[4] Through its impact on earnings, the elimination of child marriage and early childbearing would also have positive effects on welfare and poverty, because higher earnings for women would lead to higher household consumption. The impacts on earnings and poverty of universal secondary education would be even more significant. As mentioned elsewhere (World Bank 2020a), under current conditions poverty rates are not likely to be reduced substantially in coming years. Ending child marriage and early childbearing and educating girls could help change these conditions, with higher earnings ultimately pushing down poverty rates.

Agency and other impacts

A woman's capacity for choice depends on her degree of agency, which refers to her capacity to act within her environment. This capacity may be influenced by how much access she has to resources and her degree of confidence, based, among other things, on her past achievements and those of her peers and role models. Child marriage clearly affects girls' access to resources. Among other factors, access to resources may be affected by low earnings due to less education and the limits placed on girls' confidence if they have not had access to certain types of employment. Thus, child marriage clearly affects agency for girls and women. Agency can be measured in terms of a wide range of indicators, one of which is whether women are able to make decisions for the household and themselves, including seeking medical care when they need to. Some outcomes may also result from a lack of agency, such as whether mothers register their children soon after birth. Although such indicators cannot comprehensively describe women's agency, data on them are at least available in recent surveys. The direct impacts of child marriage on such indicators are typically not large and often not statistically significant; however, because child marriage and early childbearing reduce how much education girls get, they are likely to have indirect negative impacts on agency. At times, these impacts may be large, as is the case in Sierra Leone for decision-making.

Summary of the impacts

The negative impacts of child marriage, early childbearing, and low educational attainment for girls are large. Table 6.1 summarizes the estimates qualitatively; two conclusions emerge: (1) the correlations between child marriage, early childbearing, and low levels of education are strong; and (2) all three issues have negative impacts individually or collectively on a wide range of other outcomes. In addition, some of the effects are not only statistically significant but also large. Finally, in addition to the effects identified in table 6.1, girls' low level of education can be shown to have other negative effects that are not discussed in this chapter (refer to the discussion in box 6.1).

TABLE 6.1 **Statistically significant estimated impacts, by domain**

DOMAINS AND INDICATORS	CHILD MARRIAGE OR EARLY CHILDBEARING	COMPLETION OF SECONDARY EDUCATION	EITHER ONE OF THE TWO
Mutual relationships			
Child marriage/early childbearing	n.a.	Yes	Yes
Educational attainment	Yes	n.a.	Yes
Fertility and population growth			
Fertility	Yes	Yes	Yes
Population growth	Yes	Yes	Yes
Modern contraceptive use	Yes	Yes	Yes
Health and nutrition			
Under-five mortality	Yes	No	Yes
Under-five stunting	No	No	No
Demand for health care	Yes	Yes	Yes
Intimate partner violence	Likely	Likely	Likely
Work and productivity			
Labor force participation	Yes	Yes	Yes
Women's earnings	Yes	Yes	Yes
Household welfare	Yes	Yes	Yes
Women's agency			
Decision-making ability	Yes	Yes	Yes
Knowledge of HIV/AIDS	No	Yes	Yes
Birth registration	No	No	No

Source: Original estimates based in part on data from the Sierra Leone Demographic and Health Survey, 2013. Wodon (forthcoming) will provide an update using data from the 2019 survey.
Note: n.a. = not applicable.

BOX 6.1

Other impacts of the limited education of girls

Apart from the impact of educational attainment on the development outcomes considered in this chapter, a World Bank study on the cost of not educating girls globally (Wodon et al. 2018) considers a range of other outcomes. For example, women with secondary education may expect to earn almost twice as much, and those with tertiary education almost three times as much, as those with no education. Women with secondary and tertiary education report higher standards of living than those who at most completed only primary education. For example, they are less likely to state that they do not have enough money to buy food. Women's psychological well-being could also improve with more education, even though gender norms may in some cases reduce those effects. Women with secondary education report less satisfaction with basic services than women with no education, which may reflect a more realistic assessment of service quality. Achieving universal secondary education could also enable more women to display altruistic behaviors, such as volunteering, donating to charity, and helping strangers, because a tendency to participate in these activities is also correlated with higher levels of education. Secondary education is also associated with a greater likelihood that women will report being able to rely on friends when in need.

ECONOMIC COSTS AND BENEFITS: THE CASE OF CHILD MARRIAGE

Putting numbers to all the costs associated with child marriage, early childbearing, and girls' limited education is beyond the scope of this chapter, but the costs for some of the largest impacts can be approximated. Here, the focus is on the costs of child marriage and the benefits of eliminating it. Of particular interest are the benefits associated with a reduction in the population growth rate, gains in educational attainment and thereby earnings, and reductions in under-five mortality and stunting (reductions in unwanted pregnancies are an additional benefit but are not discussed here). In most cases, both immediate and longer-term gains are estimated up to 2030. This longer-term estimation accounts for the cumulative nature of some of the benefits of ending child marriage, especially for population growth. It also allows valuations to adjust for increases in standards of living (GDP per capita) over time.

Through reduced population growth, ending child marriage and early childbearing could have generated immediate annual benefits of US$19 million in purchasing power parity (PPP) in 2015, which could rise to US$367 million annually by 2030. Thus, the welfare benefits derived from reducing population growth by eliminating child marriage and early childbearing are extremely significant. These estimates should not be considered as precise because they depend on (1) econometric estimates of impacts, which have themselves standard errors, and (2) a range of debatable assumptions about costing (refer to the methodology section for a discussion). Still, they provide an order of magnitude of the costs that may result from the prevalence of child marriage and the benefits of its elimination. The estimates of costs here are based on annual losses in GDP per capita or components thereof, such as labor earnings. If lifetime losses were computed using, for example, estimates of the changing wealth of nations (Lange, Wodon, and Carey 2018), the estimates of costs would be substantially larger than those reported here (refer to, for example, Wodon and de la Brière 2018; Wodon et al. 2018). Table 6.2 gives illustrative estimates of annual benefits from ending child marriage (or, equivalently, some of the costs of inaction). The fact that the benefits increase substantially over time relates to the cumulative effect of the reduction in population growth on the country's total population over 15 years, and the gains in standards of living over the same period. This cumulative effect explains why the size of the annual benefits in 2030 are about 20 times their value in 2015.

Over time, there would also be budget savings due to reduced demand for public services as population growth is reduced. In other countries, based on a model developed by Wils (2015), the impact of the elimination of child marriage

TABLE 6.2 **Order of magnitude, selected benefits from ending child marriage (US$ PPP, unless otherwise noted)**

	ANNUAL BENEFIT IN 2015	ANNUAL BENEFIT IN 2030
Welfare benefit from reduced population growth	19 million	367 million
Benefit from reduced under-five mortality	20 million	28 million
Benefit from reduced under-five stunting	Not statistically significant	Not statistically significant
Education budget savings	None	5% or more of education budget[a]

Source: Original estimates based in part on data from the Sierra Leone Demographic and Health Survey, 2013. Wodon (forthcoming) will provide an update using data from the 2019 survey.
Note: PPP = purchasing power parity.
a. Estimate based on simulations for other similar countries.

and early childbirths on savings for the national education budget can be computed. Typically, by 2030, new cohorts of children in school would be smaller because of population growth, and the number of students in school could be reduced by at least 5 percent versus a business-as-usual scenario. The resulting savings would be valued at millions of dollars. Additional savings would be generated for the national budget, including in health.

Economic benefits would also be reaped from the reduction in under-five mortality brought about by the elimination of child marriage, and thereby a sharp reduction in early childbearing. The valuation of these benefits also rests on a number of debatable assumptions, but under standard practice the valuation of lives is related to future losses in GDP when children die prematurely. The benefits from reducing under-five mortality by 2030 are valued under such assumptions at US$20 million (PPP) in 2015, rising to US$28 million (PPP) in 2030. Because estimates of the impact of early childbearing on the risk of under-five stunting were not statistically significant, the gains in wages related to potentially lower stunting rates when ending child marriage and thereby reducing early childbearing are not estimated (refer to box 6.2 on why some estimates of the economic costs of child marriage tend to be larger than others).

In addition, the potential earnings losses due to early marriages in 2015 are estimated at US$71 million (PPP). Because child marriage reduces girls' educational attainment, early marriage also affects women's earnings in terms of how much more women who married early would have earned if they had been able

---

BOX 6.2

Why are some impacts and costs large and others smaller?

In economic terms, the fact that reducing child marriage or early childbirth may lead to only relatively small reductions in national measures for some outcomes does not imply that the associated economic costs are small. For example, in many countries, child marriage tends to reduce earnings nationally by an average of about 1 percent. A single percent may not seem to be much, but the associated economic cost is very large; and, for the women affected, the losses in earnings are much greater.

Some of the most significant economic costs associated with child marriage are related to fertility and population growth, education and earnings, and the health of the children born of young mothers. These impacts are closely related. Particularly when use of modern contraception is low, with a lack of access to safe sexual and reproductive health services, child marriage is closely correlated with early childbirth, which in turn is closely correlated with greater health risks for young mothers and the children they bear and leads to higher fertility rates. Child marriage and early childbirth make it very difficult for girls to continue their education, which cuts women's earnings potential. All those effects are at work at the time of marriage (in the case of educational attainment) or soon after (in the case of childbearing).

By contrast, impacts in other domains, such as risk of domestic violence, labor force participation, and decision-making, can be observed throughout a woman's life. They may also depend on many factors apart from whether and when girls marry. For example, intimate partner violence and a lack of decision-making ability are at least partially the result of widespread gender inequality. Although child marriage tends to perpetuate gender inequality, delaying marriage by a few years may not be enough by itself to fundamentally change gender roles and social norms. Thus, in these domains, although the elimination of child marriage may have a significant role, the impact tends to be relatively small compared to that of higher levels of girls' educational attainment, for example.

to marry later and spend more time in school. There is a significant literature on the potential impact of educational attainment on earnings, regardless of gender (for a review, refer to Psacharopoulos and Patrinos 2018). In the case of Sierra Leone, estimates by the International Monetary Fund (2020) suggest that long-term gains from closing gender gaps in education across income groups could lead to a permanent increase in GDP of about 8 percent. (The benefits of improving the quality of the education being provided could be even larger.) Because of the cost in terms of girls' education, child marriage reduces earnings throughout a woman's life. Because of data and time limitations, this chapter does not attempt to determine the impact of low educational attainment and child marriage on monetary poverty, but a global study suggests that these effects on poverty are likely to be large (UNESCO 2017). This information is important given expectations that in Sierra Leone under current conditions poverty may not decrease substantially in the near future. If child marriage were ended, poverty reduction would be accelerated substantially.

The various estimates of the cost of child marriage are substantial. To illustrate the magnitude of the benefits from ending child marriage, comparisons with net official development assistance (ODA) may be useful. ODA consists of disbursements of loans made on concessional terms (net of principal repayments) and grants by official agencies, whether or not they are members of the Development Assistance Committee; multilateral institutions; and countries not eligible for aid from the Development Assistance Committee. Net ODA includes loans, of which grant elements constitute at least 25 percent of the value. In Sierra Leone, for the past decade net ODA has fluctuated between approximately 10 and 20 percent of gross national income in recent years. Although the benefits from eliminating child marriage are smaller, they are nevertheless large as a proportion of GDP, especially for gains from lower fertility and population growth, which are cumulative over time.

OPTIONS TO IMPROVE OPPORTUNITIES FOR ADOLESCENT GIRLS

Eliminating child marriage and early childbearing and improving educational opportunities for girls could generate substantial economic benefits for Sierra Leone. There are three main reasons why investing in opportunities for adolescent girls is often highly cost-effective. First, earlier investments tend to have a persistent positive impact throughout women's lives. If a girl completes secondary education and avoids early marriage, the benefits endure throughout her life. Second, the cost of interventions for girls in adolescence or even earlier tends to be lower than the cost of interventions later in women's life cycles. Third, interventions targeted at girls at a formative age may be more successful in influencing values and behaviors, not only for the girls directly targeted but also for the community. If women are targeted later in life, returns on the investment may be lower because it becomes increasingly difficult for them to fully benefit from new opportunities. Although interventions for women at a later point in the life cycle may also be justified, adolescence is a critical development period when investments are likely to generate the highest returns.

To eliminate child marriage and early childbearing and to enable all girls to complete their secondary education, some general conditions must be met, but a number of specific interventions also have promise. The following subsections discuss these general conditions and specific interventions, acknowledging that major efforts supported by the government are already under way. The objective of the discussion in these subsections is not to lay out a comprehensive plan, because that has been done elsewhere (on child marriage and early childbearing, refer to the National Strategy for the Reduction of Adolescent Pregnancy and Child Marriage 2018–2022 [Government of Sierra Leone 2018b]; on education, including specific interventions related to girls' education, refer to the Education Sector Plan 2018–2020 [Government of Sierra Leone 2018a]). Rather, the objective is to highlight selected policies that are particularly important to improve investments in adolescent girls.

General conditions

Multiple interventions are needed to provide opportunities to girls and ensure that their needs are met.[5] Some of these interventions have already been implemented or planned by the government. In May 2013, a National Secretariat for the Reduction of Teenage Pregnancy was established, leading to the adoption of a strategy for 2013–15.[6] More recently, a National Strategy for the Reduction of Adolescent Pregnancy and Child Marriage 2018–22 was adopted, with a multisectoral approach aiming to coordinate actions from five ministries.[7] In addition, in August 2018, President Bio announced the Free Quality School Education Program initiative, with the aim of ensuring free schooling for 1.5 million children while also training thousands of teachers and providing free textbooks. Getting the most out of this new policy will require a tight focus on narrowing gender disparities in education outcomes.

On March 30, 2020, Sierra Leone overturned a ban on school attendance by pregnant girls. The ban was introduced in 2015 after the country experienced an increase in teenage pregnancies following the Ebola crisis. Immediately after the Court of Justice of the Economic Community of West African States ruled in mid-December 2019 that the ban was a violation of girls' right to education, the Ministry of Basic and Senior Secondary Education launched a multistakeholder task force on sexual and reproductive health. The end of the ban on pregnant girls in school is a major first step toward inclusive education, in which all children, regardless of class, ethnicity, tribe, disability, location, gender, or reproductive or parenting status, are able to learn in mainstream schools.

Given that one of the best ways to end child marriage and early childbearing is to keep adolescent girls in school, measures are needed to improve education outcomes. Multiple entry points are often needed to eliminate child marriage and achieve universal secondary education for girls. They include, among other things, reducing the disadvantages confronting girls in remote communities; creating a more inclusive school culture for girls; providing both boys and girls with sexual and reproductive health education; providing girls with role models, such as female teachers; and raising the returns to secondary school completion for women through local employment opportunities (refer to box 6.3 on lessons from the literature). More generally, Sierra Leone, in common with many other low-income countries, needs to improve basic general conditions in its education system so that all girls remain in school. Several such conditions are worth emphasizing here:

- *The need for an adequate schooling infrastructure and safe learning environment.* Secondary education completion rates are low in some areas in part because there are just not enough secondary schools to facilitate universal

Improving educational attainment and learning for girls

Several reviews consider interventions to improve education for girls and empower them, including Botea et al. (2017), Evans and Yuan (2022), Sperling and Winthrop (2015), Unterhalter et al. (2014), and Wodon (2018). For example, Unterhalter et al. (2014) assess the impact of interventions promoting girls' education specifically through (1) resources (such as cash transfers) and infrastructure, (2) improved institutions responding to student needs, and (3) changed social norms, especially for those affecting the most marginalized. The review summarizes the impact of different interventions on three outcomes: participation, learning, and empowerment. For each type of intervention and outcome, the evidence on the likelihood of impact is considered strong, promising, limited, or weak. For participation, the evidence for the impact of cash transfers, information about the potential employment returns to education, and the provision of schools in underserved and unsafe areas is strong. This is also true for a range of interventions related to teacher training, group learning, measures to promote girl-friendly schools, and learning outside

the classroom, such as through tutoring. Group learning, programs for learning outside the classroom, and scholarships linked to student performance are also found to have impacts on learning. The evidence for the impact of interventions on empowerment is weaker.

Evans and Yuan (2022) note that some past efforts to synthesize evidence on how to improve educational outcomes for girls have focused on interventions targeted to girls. However, nontargeted interventions benefiting both girls and boys may also improve girls' education. Looking at the evidence from a large set of interventions, the authors suggest that, to improve both access and learning for girls, girl-targeted interventions may not necessarily deliver better results than interventions that could benefit boys as well as girls and are thus not specifically targeting girls. For example, cash transfer programs may be directed to households as opposed to specifically to girls, or interventions for improved pedagogy in the classroom need not necessarily be gender-specific.

completion. Development of a school catchment area and rationalization plan is essential to bring schools closer to children's homes and reduce the distance to travel to school, which in turn would help with ensuring girls' safety on the way to school. School construction can reduce transportation costs in areas with extremely low schooling density, with particularly positive impacts for girls. Schools also need to provide access to water, sanitation, and hygiene facilities, which are important for adolescent girls—this is also an area where the government could place a renewed emphasis. Where schools cannot be constructed in locations that meet the needs of specific communities, it may be necessary to provide transportation to enable girls to attend school or implement scholarship programs that enable girls to live with host families at a reasonable cost. Finally, it is essential to ensure that girls do not suffer physical, sexual, or other harassment either at school or while traveling to and from school (refer more generally to Abramsky et al. 2014, on gender-based violence and how to reduce it in Uganda, and Mgalla, Schapink, and Boerma 1998, on a guardian program in primary schools in Tanzania with female teachers elected by colleagues and trained as guardians for female students).

- *The need to ensure that the education system delivers effective learning outcomes.* In many countries in Africa (Bashir et al. 2018), and more generally in the developing world (World Bank 2018a, 2018b), student learning outcomes, as measured by national and international student assessments, are poor.

Sierra Leone is no exception. This situation needs to be addressed through investments to ensure not just greater access but also improved quality. As summarized by the World Bank (2020a; also World Bank 2022), priorities in this area include increasing teacher numbers in line with standards and emphasizing subject areas with acute shortages (for example, mathematics and science). A stronger system of in-service teacher training should be institutionalized, and a teacher awards program could help encourage reductions in gender gaps in school performance. Providing in-service teacher training to challenge gender differences in teacher expectations and establishing teacher mentors to support girls could also help. Combining teacher incentives with additional resources to improve the learning environment has also been a successful strategy to improve outcomes in many countries. Finally, adopting a teacher deployment strategy to ensure more gender-balanced staffing in schools (that is, enough female teachers to provide role models for girls and create a more supportive learning environment) is also a promising approach. Guidance on these and other teacher policies is available (Beteille and Evans, 2018; on Sierra Leone, refer to World Bank 2022.).

- *The need to ensure the participation of girls.* Schooling must be affordable for girls' families. Affordability refers not just to the direct costs of participation in secondary education but also to opportunity costs. In Sierra Leone, as in neighboring low-income countries, these various costs, including expenditures for school uniforms, may remain too high for the poor. The government's Free Quality School Education Program is a major step forward, yet it will be important to ensure that the necessary budget resources to implement the policy will be made available, which may be challenging in the current economic environment affected by the COVID-19 global crisis. Providing secondary education free of tuition and other direct costs may also not be enough to ensure the participation of all school-age children, particularly girls (refer to Koski et al. 2018). Sierra Leone already has some experience with conditional cash transfer programs, but such programs could be expanded to provide greater coverage of poor households, cover more of the secondary school costs for girls, and open nonformal pathways to return to school or pursue education. Also of interest are programs run by nongovernmental organizations in Sierra Leone as well as other countries to cover the direct and indirect costs of schooling for girls while also supporting community-led initiatives to engage parents and train teacher mentors, staff, and parents to improve educational quality through low-cost educational resources (more broadly, refer to Delprato et al. 2017 for the case of the Campaign for Female Education).

In addition to reforms to policies related directly to education, broader efforts are required to change social norms that perpetuate gender inequality. The importance of social norms is noted in Sierra Leone's National Strategy for the Reduction of Adolescent Pregnancy and Child Marriage 2018–2022. Although extensive discussion of the issue of social norms is beyond the scope of this chapter, it must be recognized that child marriage, early childbearing, and low educational attainment for girls are part of deep-seated patterns of gender inequality (Klugman et al. 2014). Broad reforms are needed to change these social norms and address other constraints that limit opportunities for girls. The Convention on the Rights of the Child emphasizes the need for full and informed consent to marriage, noting that children do not have the capability to provide such consent. This is one of the reasons why 18 is recommended as the minimum age for marriage. In Sierra Leone, the Child Rights Act 2007 prohibits marriage for anyone under the age of 18, but it is undermined by the Customary Marriage Act 2007, which allows marriage under 18 with parental consent. Although enforcing laws to this effect is an important step in the right direction, as noted by Wodon et al. (2017), most child marriages take place below the national legal minimum age, demonstrating that simply passing laws is not enough (on difficulties in enforcing child marriage laws in the case of Sierra Leone, refer to Plan UK 2013).

Specific interventions

It is essential that countries promulgate appropriate laws to facilitate the elimination of child marriage; however, specific strategies and interventions to empower girls are also required. In particular, interventions are required to ensure that girls have appropriate life skills and knowledge of sexual and reproductive health (SRH). Economic incentives may also be needed so that girls can afford to remain in school, return to school if they drop out, or expand their livelihood opportunities if they cannot return.

To facilitate selection of interventions, the following subsections summarize international evidence related to three categories of interventions for adolescent girls: (1) programs that provide girls with life skills and reproductive health knowledge, (2) programs that expand girls' economic opportunities, and (3) programs designed to ensure that girls remain in school or that enable them to return to school. Each type of program is based on a different theory of change (box 6.4). The summary of findings provided here is based on a review by Botea et al. (2017) of almost 40 interventions. To qualify for review, interventions had to (1) target girls ages 10–19, either exclusively or as part of a larger group; (2) equip girls with life skills and SRH knowledge, economic opportunities, or educational opportunities; (3) demonstrate results in terms of improving the health of young women, especially SRH, or delaying marriage or childbearing; and (4) have been tested in a developing country, usually in Sub-Saharan Africa but also in other low-income settings such as Bangladesh or parts of India (refer also to Kalamar, Lee-Rife, and Hindin 2016, for another review of the international evidence).

Empowering girls

A first category of interventions emphasizes empowerment of girls by providing them with life skills and SRH knowledge. One typical intervention is provision of SRH education. In Sierra Leone, comprehensive sexual education has been developed to be incorporated in school curricula and will be rolled out soon. In many developing countries, including Sierra Leone, adolescent girls are less likely than older women to access SRH services, including modern contraception and skilled assistance during pregnancy and childbirth. Only 4.5 percent of the young female population in Sierra Leone reported that they used a condom during intercourse in the past 12 months, which was less than a third of the proportion of the young male population's condom use (15.4 percent). As discussed earlier, child marriage and educational attainment have an impact on modern contraceptive use. International evidence shows that SRH knowledge would generate multiple benefits, enabling girls to stay healthy, make independent decisions about their health, avoid unintended pregnancies, finish their education, engage in productive work, and choose to have fewer and healthier babies, when they are ready.

Another intervention is to provide a "safe space club" for adolescent girls. These clubs convene girls under the guidance of a trusted adult mentor at a

BOX 6.4

Theories of change for interventions targeting adolescent girls

Life skills and sexual and reproductive health knowledge. By increasing their knowledge, life skills can raise girls' awareness of the risks associated with becoming pregnant at an early age and increase their desire and ability to avoid early pregnancies through family planning. Through such channels, life skills may lead to better health outcomes for the girls and their children. By increasing girls' confidence and self-esteem, life skills may also help expand their aspirations, which may heighten their motivation to delay marriage and childbearing. Finally, life skills can increase the communication and decision-making skills of young women and increase their abilities to negotiate their marriage and childbearing preferences. However, although life skills and sexual and reproductive health knowledge may empower girls, they may not be sufficient to delay marriage and childbearing if social norms curtailing the agency of girls are not also addressed.

Life skills and economic opportunities. Programs to increase young women's earnings potential may increase their ability to plan and improve their marriage and childbearing decisions in three ways. First, improving a woman's ability to make an economic contribution expands her role beyond that of sex and reproduction, which can increase a girl's desire to delay marriage or childbearing. The transformation of girls from economic liabilities into assets in the eyes of their communities and families can also alleviate the external pressures on them to marry or have children early. Second, the loss in earnings associated with childrearing is an opportunity cost that may increase women's desire to limit or space births and to exercise reproductive control. Finally, increased earnings may supplement a young woman's bargaining power within the household and allow her to effectively exercise reproductive control by negotiating delays in sexual debut or marriage and to better negotiate the terms of sex, such as use of contraceptives. Creating income-generating opportunities for women can therefore, in addition to the direct economic benefit, contribute to female empowerment by widening a woman's personal choice and control over sexual and reproductive outcomes.

Incentives for girls to participate in schooling or delay marriage. In many communities, the economic, cultural, and social environment does not offer adolescent girls viable alternatives to marriage. Once girls drop out of school, possibly because of the school's poor quality or high cost, parents may find it difficult to identify any option other than marrying off their daughters. In such communities, providing better-quality and affordable primary and secondary education may be one of the best ways to delay marriage and childbearing. Programs to keep girls in school may also lead to tipping points in communities that make it easier for more and more girls to stay in school and thus delay marriage. A few interventions have also aimed to delay marriage by providing financial incentives conditional on not marrying early, with additional schooling often a benefit.

Source: Botea et al. 2017.

specific time and place. Such clubs have proven effective when they are implemented well. By combining opportunities to socialize and have fun with access to mentors, the clubs are attractive to girls and offer a platform for other services. Clubs can be held in a variety of settings, often schools or community centers. Girls are able to discuss a range of issues under the guidance of the mentors, including those related to SRH. The clubs facilitate the delivery of life skills, including "soft" or socioemotional skills such as critical thinking and problem solving, negotiation, and communication (for example within a girl's household). One of the objectives is often to boost the self-awareness and self-esteem of girls so that they can explore and fulfill their own aspirations. Often, safe space clubs are also used to facilitate the delivery of "hard" skills such as basic literacy and numeracy, or basic business skills.

These programs have helped to improve girls' SRH knowledge and behaviors. Outcomes have included increases in girls undergoing HIV testing or counseling; greater use of modern contraception or other methods of family planning; a reduction in the desire for female genital mutilation for daughters in countries where the practice is prevalent; a reduced risk of intimate partner violence when a program also reaches out to men; higher self-esteem; and gains in specific skills taught in safe space sessions, such as financial and basic literacy and numeracy.

However, without additional supportive interventions to enable girls to participate in schooling or employment or otherwise improve their livelihood options, it is not clear that safe spaces alone can delay marriage and childbearing (perhaps because that may not have been a primary goal for a club). Therefore, it is important to consider programs that combine safe spaces with measures to improve livelihood opportunities or offer incentives to remain in school, which are usually more effective in delaying marriage and childbearing.

Providing employment opportunities

The second category of programs emphasizes both empowering girls, often through safe spaces, and providing livelihood opportunities. These programs are particularly appropriate for girls who are not in school and would otherwise have no income-generating skills. Two groups of interventions are distinguished: (1) livelihood interventions and (2) interventions to improve financial literacy and access to financial services. Impacts in terms of delaying marriage and childbearing generally (though not always) tend to be larger than for the life skills/SRH knowledge programs alone.

These programs often have some success in terms of increasing the earnings, employment, or savings of girls. Several programs in other countries have also resulted in increased use of modern contraceptives and improved SRH knowledge, which may help to delay childbearing. Some have also succeeded in delaying age at marriage and in reducing teen pregnancies. For example, the Bangladesh Rehabilitation Assistance Committee's Uganda Empowerment and Livelihoods for Adolescent Girls program helped increase the likelihood of girls engaging in income-generating and self-reported routine condom use, while reducing the share of girls sexually active, decreasing fertility rates, and decreasing the number of reports of unwanted sex. There were also reductions in teenage pregnancies and child marriage, and a shift in community gender dynamics (Bandiera et al. 2020). Clearly, adding a livelihood dimension to life skills and SRH knowledge programs may help delay marriage and childbearing. The focus on economic opportunities may also help to ensure the regular participation of girls in the programs.

Providing incentives to keep girls in school

The third set of programs focuses on specific interventions to ensure that girls remain in school, enable them to return if they have dropped out, or directly delay marriage. There have been numerous interventions to keep girls in school and delay marriage (Kalamar, Lee-Rife, and Hindin 2016). In a few cases, evaluations also demonstrate that programs that provide incentives for girls to remain in school often succeed in delaying marriage or childbearing. Although most of these programs are designed to keep girls in school, some are also designed to enable girls who dropped out to return to school.

Conditional cash transfers may also be effective in incentivizing girls' schooling, promoting health, and supporting families during shocks. These incentives are often conditional on children's attendance at school or participation in preventive medicine programs. A significant body of research shows that such transfers have been effective in promoting participation in schooling by children in developing countries. The programs have been introduced in more than 29 low-income countries. Cash transfers without conditions and income support programs have also had numerous positive outcomes, such as reduced child labor, expanding schooling, and enhancing childhood nutrition (Bastagli et al. 2019). Although not all programs succeed everywhere, the evidence is quite convincing that, in comparison to the other two types of programs reviewed in the preceding subsections, those focusing directly on schooling for girls, or in some cases using financial incentives to delay marriage, may be more successful in delaying marriage and childbearing.

Summary for targeted interventions

The three types of interventions described are not intended to be an exhaustive list. To improve girls' educational attainment, additional interventions may also be needed. The three types of interventions were selected because there is evidence that they help improve SRH knowledge and delay child marriage and early childbearing. The programs and interventions are also not mutually exclusive; implemented together, they can complement each other. Although some programs are better than others in achieving the desired goals, all three categories of programs may have significant benefits of many kinds. With different interventions targeting different groups of girls (for example, those in school or with the potential to return to school and those who dropped out and may not be able to return), all three categories should be considered when formulating a strategy to improve opportunities for adolescent girls. Another example is associating cash transfers with measures to boost girls' agency, for example through building soft skills and promoting learning about nutrition and reproductive health (World Bank 2012).

CONCLUSION

Investments to eliminate child marriage and early childbearing and promote education for girls should not be based solely on economic considerations, but the economic benefits of doing so would be large. The primary motivation for eliminating child marriage and early childbearing and promoting education for girls should be to address the substantial risks and suffering that confront adolescent girls and their children. The risks faced by adolescent girls are particularly salient, as evidenced by the recent COVID-19 crisis. However, this chapter demonstrates that, in addition to these benefits, the economic benefits to Sierra Leone from such investments would be significant—and the costs of failing to address related issues are proportionately high. Demonstrating the magnitude of these costs provides additional justification for investments in adolescent girls. Although further work is needed to identify the best policy options for Sierra Leone to improve opportunities for adolescent girls, useful lessons can be learned from international experience. Ending child marriage, preventing early childbearing, and improving education opportunities for girls not only are the right things to do from a moral and ethical standpoint but also represent a smart investment for the country's development.

NOTES

1. The Department for International Development supported Sierra Leone Secondary Education Learning Assessments in 2017 and 2018.
2. The estimates for Sierra Leone are based on an extrapolation of results for other countries where simulations were conducted using demographic projection tools. Comparison with impacts on fertility rates suggest that the estimates are as expected.
3. Under-five mortality was highest among children of mothers who were younger than age 20 at the time of the birth (136 deaths per 1,000 live births).
4. The estimates for Sierra Leone are based on an extrapolation of results for other countries where simulations were conducted using labor force surveys.
5. It is beyond the scope of this report to provide a comprehensive analysis of what needs to be done to end child marriage and early childbearing and to ensure that all girls complete secondary education, but pointers are provided.
6. The Ebola outbreak in 2014 did not allow the implementation of the strategy, and it was particularly detrimental to girls' education. Schools were closed for almost an entire year, leading to higher risks of unwanted and transactional sex for food and other essentials. In part as a result, more than 18,000 girls became pregnant (UNFPA 2017). When schools reopened, girls were 16 percentage points less likely to be in school (Bandiera et al. 2019).
7. Ministry of Health and Sanitation; Ministry of Social Welfare, Gender, and Children's Affairs; Ministry of Basic and Senior Secondary Education; Ministry of Local Government and Rural Development; and the Ministry of Youth Affairs.

REFERENCES

Abramsky, T., K. Devries, L. Kiss, J. Nakuti, N. Kyegombe, E. Starmann, B. Cundill, L. Francisco, D. Kaye, T. Musuya, L. Michau, and C. Watts. 2014. "Findings from the SASA! Study: A Cluster Randomized Controlled Trial to Assess the Impact of a Community Mobilization Intervention to Prevent Violence against Women and Reduce HIV Risk in Kampala, Uganda." *BMC Medicine* 12: 122.

Acemoglu, D. 2010. "Theory, General Equilibrium and Political Economy." NBER Working Paper 15944, National Bureau of Economic Research, Cambridge, MA.

Acemoglu, D., D. H. Autor, and D. Lyle. 2004. "Women, War, and Wages: The Effect of Female Labor Supply on the Wage Structure at Midcentury." *Journal of Political Economy* 112 (3): 497–551.

Angrist, J. D. 1995. "The Economic Returns to Schooling in the West Bank and Gaza." *American Economic Review* 85 (5): 1065–87.

Bandiera, O., N. Buehren, M. Goldstein, I. Rasul, and A. Smurra. 2019. "The Economic Lives of Young Women in the Time of Ebola: Lessons from an Empowerment Program." Policy Research Working Paper 8760, World Bank, Washington, DC.

Bandiera, O., N. Buehren, R. Burgess, M. Goldstein, S. Gulesci, I. Rasul, and M. Sulaiman. 2020. "Women's Empowerment in Action: Evidence from a Randomized Control Trial in Africa." *American Economic Journal: Applied Economics* 12 (1): 210–59.

Bashir, S., M. Lockheed, E. Ninan, and J.-P. Tan. 2018. *Facing Forward: Schooling for Learning in Africa*. Washington, DC: World Bank.

Bastagli, F., J. Hagen-Zanker, L. Harman, V. Barca, G. Sturge, and T. Schmidt. 2019. "The Impact of Cash Transfers: A Review of the Evidence from Low- and Middle-Income Countries." *Journal of Social Policy* 48 (3): 569–94.

Beteille, T., and D. Evans. 2018. *Successful Teachers, Successful Students: Recruiting and Supporting Society's Most Crucial Profession*. Washington, DC: World Bank.

Black, M. M., S. P. Walker, L. C. H. Fernald, C. T. Andersen, A. M. DiGirolamo, C. Lu, D. C. McCoy, G. Fink, Y. R. Shawar, J. Shiffman, A. E. Devercelli, Q. T. Wodon, E. Vargas-Baron, and S. Grantham-McGregor. 2017. "Early Childhood Development Coming of Age: Science through the Life Course." *Lancet* 389 (10064): 77–90.

Botea, I., S. Chakravarty, S. Haddock, and Q. Wodon. 2017. *Interventions Improving Sexual and Reproductive Health Outcomes and Delaying Child Marriage and Childbearing for Adolescent Girls*. Ending Child Marriage Notes Series. Washington, DC: World Bank.

Canning, D., S. Raja, and A. S. Yazbeck. 2015. *Africa's Demographic Transition Dividend or Disaster?* Washington, DC: World Bank.

Delprato, M., B. Alcott, P. Rose, and R. Sabates. 2017. "Analysing Cost-Effectiveness of Raising Learning for Marginalised Girls through CAMFED's Programme: A Methodological Note." REAL Centre, University of Cambridge, Cambridge, UK.

Duflo, E. 2004. "The Medium Run Effects of Educational Expansion: Evidence from a Large School Construction Program in Indonesia." *Journal of Development Economics* 74 (1): 163–97.

Evans, D. K., and F. Yuan. 2022. "What We Learn about Girls' Education from Interventions That Do Not Focus on Girls." *World Bank Economic Review* 36 (1): 244–67.

Field, E., and A. Ambrus. 2008. "Early Marriage, Age of Menarche, and Female Schooling Attainment in Bangladesh." *Journal of Political Economy* 116 (5): 881–930.

Government of Sierra Leone. 2018a. *Education Sector Plan 2018–20*. Freetown: Government of Sierra Leone.

Government of Sierra Leone. 2018b. *National Strategy for the Reduction of Adolescent Pregnancy and Child Marriage 2018–2022*. Freetown: Government of Sierra Leone.

Hoddinott, J., J. R. Behrman, J. A. Maluccio, P. Melgar, A. R. Quisumbing, M. Ramirez Zea, A. D. Stein, K. M. Yount, and R. Martorell. 2013. "Adult Consequences of Growth Failure in Early Childhood." *American Journal of Clinical Nutrition* 98 (5): 1170–8.

Horton, S., and R. Steckel. 2013. "Global Economic Losses Attributable to Malnutrition 1900–2000 and Projections to 2050." In *The Economics of Human Challenges*, edited by B. Lomborg, 247–72. Cambridge, U.K: Cambridge University Press.

International Monetary Fund. 2020. *Sierra Leone: Selected Issues*. IMF Country Report No. 20/117. Washington, DC: International Monetary Fund.

Kalamar, A. M., S. Lee-Rife, and M. J. Hindin. 2016. "Interventions to Prevent Child Marriage among Young People in Low- and Middle-Income Countries: A Systematic Review of the Published and Gray Literature." *Journal of Adolescent Health* 59: S16–S21.

Klugman, J., L. Hanmer, S. Twigg, T. Hasan, J. McCleary-Sills, and J. Santamaria. 2014. *Voice and Agency: Empowering Women and Girls for Shared Prosperity*. Washington, DC: World Bank.

Koski, A., E. C. Strumpf, J. S. Kaufman, J. Frank, J. Heymann, and A. Nandi. 2018. "The Impact of Eliminating Primary School Tuition Fees on Child Marriage in Sub-Saharan Africa: A Quasi-Experimental Evaluation of Policy Changes in 8 Countries." *PLoS One* 13 (5): e0197928.

Lange, G. M., Q. Wodon, and K. Carey. 2018. *The Changing Wealth of Nations 2018: Sustainability into the 21st Century*. Washington, DC: World Bank.

Male, C., and Q. Wodon. 2018. "Girls' Education and Child Marriage in West and Central Africa: Trends, Impacts, Costs, and Solutions." *Forum for Social Economics* 47 (2): 262–74.

Mgalla, Z., D. Schapink, and J. T. Boerma. 1998. "Protecting School Girls against Sexual Exploitation: A Guardian Programme in Mwanza, Tanzania." *Reproductive Health Matters* 6 (12): 19–30.

Nguyen, M. C., and Q. Wodon. 2014. "Impact of Child Marriage on Literacy and Educational Attainment in Africa." Background Paper for *Fixing the Broken Promise of Education for All*, UNESCO Institute of Statistics and UNICEF, Paris and New York.

Nove, A., Z. Matthews, S. Neal, and A. V. Camacho. 2014. "Maternal Mortality in Adolescents Compared with Women of Other Ages: Evidence from 144 Countries." *Lancet Global Health* 2 (3): 155–64.

Onagoruwa, A., and Q. Wodon. 2018. "Measuring the Impact of Child Marriage on Total Fertility: Study for Fifteen Countries." *Journal of Biosocial Science* 50 (5): 626–39.

Onyango, M. A., K. Resnick, A. Davis, and R. R. Shah. 2019. "Gender-Based Violence among Adolescent Girls and Young Women: A Neglected Consequence of the West African Ebola Outbreak." In *Pregnant in the Time of Ebola*, edited by D. A. Schwartz, J. N. Anoko, and S. A. Abramowitz, 121–32. Cham: Springer.

Plan UK (Plan United Kingdom). 2013. "Before Their Time: Challenges to Implementing the Prohibition against Child Marriage in Sierra Leone." Plan UK, London.

Psacharopoulos, G., and H. A. Patrinos. 2018. "Returns to Investment in Education: A Decennial Review of the Global Literature." *Education Economics* 26 (5): 445–58.

Savadogo, A., and Q. Wodon. 2018. *Impact of Child Marriage on Women's Earnings across Multiple Countries.* Washington, DC: World Bank.

Sperling, G., and R. Winthrop. 2015. *What Works in Girls' Education: Evidence for the World's Best Investment.* Washington, DC: Brookings Institution.

Street Child. 2016. *Girls Speak Out: The Street Child National Consultation on Adolescent Girls' Education in Sierra Leone.* Freetown: Street Child.

UNESCO (United Nations Educational, Scientific and Cultural Organization). 2017. "Reducing Global Poverty through Universal Primary and Secondary Education." Policy Paper 32/Fact Sheet 44, UNESCO, Paris.

UNFPA (United Nations Population Fund). 2017. *Recovering from the Ebola Virus Disease: Rapid Assessment of Pregnant Adolescent Girls in Sierra Leone.* Freetown, Sierra Leone: UNFPA.

United Nations. 2020. *Policy Brief: The Impact of COVID-19 on Children.* New York: United Nations.

Unterhalter, E., A. North, M. Arnot, C. Lloyd, L. Moletsane, E. Murphy-Graham, J. Parkes, and M. Saito. 2014. *Girls' Education and Gender Equality.* London: Department for International Development.

Wils, A. 2015. "Reaching Education Targets in Low and Lower-Middle-Income Countries: Costs and Finance Gaps to 2030." Background Paper Prepared for the UNESCO Education for All Global Monitoring Report, UNESCO, Paris.

Wodon, Q. 2016. "Early Childhood Development in the Context of the Family: The Case of Child Marriage." *Journal of Human Development and Capabilities* 17 (4): 590–8.

Wodon, Q. 2018. "Education Budget Savings from Ending Child Marriage and Early Childbirths: The Case of Niger." *Applied Economics Letters* 25 (10): 649–52.

Wodon, Q., ed. Forthcoming. *Sierra Leone: Educating Girls and Ending Child Marriage— Investment Case and the Role of Teachers and School Leaders.* Addis Ababa: UNESCO International Institute for Capacity Building in Africa.

Wodon, Q., and B. de la Brière. 2018. *Unrealized Potential: The High Cost of Gender Inequality in Earnings.* The Cost of Gender Inequality Notes Series. Washington, DC: World Bank.

Wodon, Q., C. Male, A. Nayihouba, A. Onagoruwa, A. Savadogo, A. Yedan, J. Edmeades, A. Kes, N. John, L. Murithi, M. Steinhaus, and S. Petroni. 2017. *Economic Impacts of Child Marriage: Global Synthesis Report.* Washington, DC: World Bank and International Center for Research on Women.

Wodon, Q., C. Male, and A. Onagoruwa. 2020. "A Simple Approach to Measuring the Share of Early Childbirths Likely Due to Child Marriage in Developing Countries." *Forum for Social Economics* 49 (2): 166–79.

Wodon, Q., C. Montenegro, H. Nguyen, and A. Onagoruwa. 2018. *Missed Opportunities: The High Cost of Not Educating Girls.* The Cost of Not Educating Girls Notes Series. Washington, DC: World Bank.

Wodon, Q., C. Nguyen, and C. Tsimpo. 2016. "Child Marriage, Education, and Agency in Uganda." *Feminist Economist* 22 (1): 54–79.

World Bank. 2012. *World Development Report 2012: Gender Equality and Development.* Washington, DC: World Bank.

World Bank. 2015. *Global Monitoring Report 2015/16: Development Goals in an Era of Demographic Change.* Washington, DC: World Bank.

World Bank. 2018a. "The Human Capital Project." World Bank, Washington, DC.

World Bank. 2018b. *World Development Report 2018: Learning to Realize Education's Promise.* Washington, DC: World Bank.

World Bank. 2020a. *Sierra Leone Economic Update: The Power of Investing in Girls.* Washington, DC: World Bank.

World Bank. 2020b. *The COVID-19 Pandemic: Shocks to Education and Policy Responses.* Washington, DC: World Bank.

World Bank. 2022. *Teachers and Teaching in Sierra Leone.* Washington, DC: World Bank.